What Others are Saying About this Book . . .

Walking Like Jesus Did *is a gem. This is a primer on the practical details of living the Christian life. Whether used as a discipleship manual by new Christians or an encouragement for mature saints, this book will stimulate Christlike living. This will be a valuable tool for small group use or one-on-one mentoring.*

Tedd Tripp, author of *Shepherding a Child's Heart*
Pastor, Conference Speaker

Larry McCall has contributed a timeless treasure to the Christian world in this work. I wish every believer desiring to obey Christ could read this wonderful work. It is solidly biblical and a source of inspiration as well as instruction. I highly recommend it!

Olan Hendrix
Leadership Resource Group
Powell, Ohio

While many authors have written volumes on leadership, Dr. Larry McCall and his writing challenge us with leading like Jesus did. This work has changed my life and continues to do so! If you have been called to a leadership role there is no greater leader to follow than the Son of God! Let me encourage you to keep this work by your desk, your bedside, and most importantly in your heart! A must-read to all in leadership roles!

Rod K. Mayer, President and Co-Founder
DVO Extremity Solutions LLC.

Into a world that often asks the question "What Would Jesus Do?" and then goes on its merry way, Larry McCall leads us to look repeatedly at the more basic question: "How can we be like Jesus?" Is there a difference? You bet there is! It is character that counts, specifically the character of Jesus Christ. Actions must arise from character, to please the Lord. In chapter after chapter of this book we have the Lord Jesus displayed to us so that we can absorb and reflect His character. Larry helps us visualize the people who move across his pages, leaving us with gripping mental pictures as well as words. It is a pleasure to commend both the book and its author.

Tom Wells, Pastor, King's Chapel
West Chester (Greater Cincinnati), Ohio

In a day of many "secrets" on how to live, we sometimes miss the obvious. Larry McCall drives us back to the foundations of Christian maturity summed up in the words, "Walk as Jesus Did." How true! And how relevant! If we miss this, we've missed it all.

Jim Elliff, Author, Pastor, Conference & Radio Speaker
President, Christian Communicators Worldwide
Kansas City, Missouri

Becoming like Jesus Christ began growing as a passion in my life about 35 years ago. It is an immeasurable privilege to recommend Larry McCall's profound presentation of the character of our Lord. Over the years this book could have been used hundreds of times in my pastoral counseling and discipleship to point struggling people to God's perfect standard for us—Jesus Christ, His Son.

Roger Peugh, Co-Author *Transformed in His Presence – The Need for Prayer in Counseling*
Associate Professor of World Missions,
Grace Theological Seminary
Winona Lake, Indiana

Anyone who is serious about his walk with Christ should read and put into practice the principles Pastor Larry McCall has set down in his book, Walking Like Jesus Did. *Larry has lived out these principles in his personal and pastoral life. Therefore, it is a work of practical importance to each of us believers!*

Tom Lutz, Pastor, Edgewood Baptist Church
Anderson, Indiana

Here's a wonderful treatment of an important subject that every Christian ultimately must master. Larry McCall is uniquely qualified to write about Christian maturity and Christlikeness. I appreciate the gentleness and grace that always colors his teaching, his conversation, and his pastoral ministry. That Christlike spirit comes through in his writing, and it provides a vivid, living example that makes this an extremely powerful study.

Phillip R. Johnson, Executive Director
Grace To You
Panorama City, California

WALKING LIKE JESUS DID

Studies in the Character of Christ

This is how we know we are in Him:
Whoever claims to live in Him,
must walk as Jesus did.
1 John 2:5b-6

Dr. Larry E. McCall

BMH BOOKS
Winona Lake, Indiana
www.bmhbooks.com

WALKING LIKE JESUS DID
Studies in the Character of Christ

ISBN 10: 0-88469-303-1
ISBN 13: 978-0-88469-303-1
Printed in the United States of America

Published by BMH Books
BMH Books, P.O. Box 544, Winona Lake, IN 46590 USA
www.bmhbooks.com

DEDICATION

This book is lovingly dedicated to my parents, Carl and Connie McCall, who for decades have consistently reflected Christ in their small Pennsylvania coal mining community. I believe I speak not only for their children and grandchildren, but for scores of people whose lives have been impacted by their simple but profound example of Christlikeness. I thank God for them.

Dad and Mom, thank you showing me what "walking like Jesus did" looks like in everyday life. I am eternally grateful.

ACKNOWLEDGEMENTS

Over the last twenty years, it has been my deep joy to preach and teach on the subject of "walking like Jesus did." Of the many people who have joined me in these life-challenging studies in the character of Christ, two in particular have encouraged me to put this teaching into print. For years, they have prayed for me and encouraged me to fulfill the commission of writing this book. My deep appreciation goes to my precious wife, Gladine, and to Rod Mayer, my long time friend and spiritual accountability partner.

This book also has on it the fingerprints of several gracious and competent friends who volunteered their precious time to help me sharpen and clarify the content. My thanks go to Susan Hight, Dee Woods, Don Clemens, and Steve Smilay. Lord willing, their efforts will help this book be more useful in the lives of the readers.

Terry White, the senior editor of BMH books, and his faithful team have been an encouragement to me in seeing this writing project come to fruition. They are friends as well as co-workers in the Lord's service.

But most of all, I thank my Lord Jesus Christ, "who loved me and gave himself for me" (Galatians 2:20). May in some small way, my life be a reflection of His glory as I seek, by His grace, to walk as He walked. And may this book by used by the Lord to encourage others to be faithful in this journey.

Larry McCall
Winona Lake, Indiana
November 2005

FOREWORD

Jerry Bridges

The New Testament is quite clear that God's ultimate objective for all believers is conformity to the likeness of Jesus Christ. The Apostle Paul wrote in Romans 8:29 that God predestined us to be conformed to the image or likeness of His Son. Having predestined us to that end, God sets about to transform us into that image through His Spirit at work in us (2 Corinthians 3:18). Then the writer of Hebrews tells us that the purpose of God's fatherly discipline in our lives is that we may share in His holiness. That's simply another way of saying we are being conformed to His image.

The process of conforming us to the image of Jesus Christ is usually called sanctification. It is a process carried on by the Holy Spirit but involving the intentional response and cooperation of the believer. All of the moral and ethical imperatives of Scripture assume the necessity of response on our part. And it is usually to these imperatives that we who are teachers of Scripture turn when we want to address the issues of daily Christian living.

In this book, *Walking Like Jesus Did*, Larry McCall reminds us of another dimension of biblical teaching that is designed to further our sanctification—the example of Jesus as He lived among the people of His day.

Sad to say, the example of Jesus' walk among us has often been overlooked or even dismissed among the evangelical sector of the Church. This has no doubt been a reaction to the message of those who deny the deity of Jesus and His substitutionary atonement for our sins but who teach that He was a good man whose example we should follow. As a result, we who rightly stress the objective work of Christ and His atoning sacrifice have tended to shy away from teaching that Jesus' life is an example for us to follow.

The Bible, however, does not do this. In the incident of washing His disciples' feet, Jesus Himself said, "For I have given you an example that you should do just as I have done to you" (John 13:15). And the Apostle Peter wrote of Christ's suffering for us: "Leaving you an example so that you might follow in His steps" (1 Peter 2:21).

These two Scriptures should cast aside any doubt that we believers should pay attention to the life of Jesus so that we might follow His example.

Most of us are familiar with the WWJD slogan—"What would Jesus do?" Unfortunately, the question phrased that way opens the possibility for all kinds of subjective answers. What I think Jesus would have done in a specific situation may differ from what you think He would have done.

Pastor McCall has, in effect, helpfully rephrased that question as "What *did* Jesus do?" By giving us a sort of videotaping of Jesus in action in 14 different settings, he helps us answer that question so that we have concrete examples of what it means to walk like Jesus did.

One of the strengths of this book is that it takes us outside the realm of what we normally think of as Christian character. We see Jesus on a mission; and by His example, we are challenged to live purposeful lives as "people on a mission" ourselves. We see Jesus at prayer; and again, by His example, we are convicted of our own mediocre prayer lives. We see Jesus washing the feet of His disciples and learn what it means to serve others.

I have been personally challenged by this book to pay more attention to the actions of Jesus as recorded in the Gospels and to learn from them how I might more and more walk like He did. I trust this book will have a similar impact on all who read it.

— Jerry Bridges

Jerry Bridges is a staff member with the Navigator collegiate ministry group. A prolific and best-selling author, his most recent books include The Gospel for Real Life *(2002) and* Growing Your Faith *(2004) both by NavPress.*

WALKING LIKE JESUS DID

Studies in The Character of Christ

This is how we know we are in Him:
*Whoever claims to live in Him **must walk as Jesus did**.*
(1 John 2:5b-6)

Introduction: Walking in the Footsteps of Jesus 1

Chapter 1 .... Why Walk Like Jesus Did? 5

Chapter 2 .... Walking in Meekness Like Jesus Did 13

Chapter 3 .... Walking with a Mission Like Jesus Did 21

Chapter 4 .... Living Incarnationally Like Jesus Did 29

Chapter 5 .... Walking in Holiness Like Jesus Did 37

Chapter 6 .... Accepting Others Like Jesus Did 45

Chapter 7 .... Having Compassion Like Jesus Did 55

Chapter 8 .... Suffering Like Jesus Did 65

Chapter 9 .... Persevering Like Jesus Did 75

Chapter 10 .... Practicing Patience Like Jesus Did 83

Chapter 11 .... Forgiving Like Jesus Did 91

Chapter 12 .... Praying Like Jesus Did 99

Chapter 13 .... Serving Like Jesus Did 109

Chapter 14 .... Experiencing Joy Like Jesus Did 115

Chapter 15 .... Loving Like Jesus Did 127

Chapter 16 .... The Cost of Walking Like Jesus Did 134

Chapter 17 .... The Reward of Walking Like Jesus Did 141

WALKING IN THE FOOTSTEPS OF JESUS

Imagine that there is a new person at your work or school. He is an immigrant from Abu Dhabi, and his name is Abdul. There are very few Christians in Abu Dhabi. In fact, Abdul never personally met a Christian until he moved into this new community. Since his arrival, he has overheard a number of people saying things about "so-and-so being a Christian" or "so-and-so not being a Christian."

One day on break, Abdul asks if he can talk with you. He asks if *you* are a Christian. You assure him that you are, indeed. Then he asks, "Is *everyone* in America a Christian?" You sadly admit to him, "No, not everyone in America is a Christian. In fact, Abdul, not even everyone who claims to be a Christian is one in actuality."

Then your new friend, Abdul, asks this probing question: "Well then, how can I tell who is *really* a Christian and who is *not*?" How will you answer this crucially important question? What will you say to Abdul?

Here is some help right from the Word of God. 1 John 2:3-6 explains, "We know that we have come to know him if we obey his commands. The man who says, 'I know him,' but does not do what he commands is a liar, and the truth is not in him. But if anyone obeys his word, God's love is truly made complete in him. This is how we know we are in him: Whoever claims to live in him must walk as Jesus did."

With solid footing on this part of God's Word, you can explain to Abdul that he can recognize a true follower of Jesus

Christ by these two factors: first, does the person obey Jesus' words (verses 3-5a)? Second, does this person follow in the steps of Jesus' life? Does this person "walk as Jesus did" (verses 5b-6)?

This book is a humble attempt to help those who claim to be Christians better understand what it means to "walk like Jesus did." Our *claim* ("I'm a Christian") must be matched by our *conduct* (walking like Jesus did). The true test comes in evaluating how clearly our daily lives are a reflection of the character of Jesus Christ, the One we claim to be following. Mirroring the character of Jesus should be the normal pattern of life for the Christian as he or she goes about everyday life at work, at school, in the neighborhood, and at home.

In these chapters we will focus on certain character traits Jesus demonstrated during His earthly ministry. We will also explore explicit biblical commands to mirror those character traits of Jesus in our daily lives.

My heartfelt desire is not for the reader to lay down this book and say, "That was nice." Instead, my hope and prayer is that each reader finish reading this book and say, "Lord, change me! Mold me and make me to be increasingly more like Jesus, so that I can impact my family, my church and my community for *Your* fame!"

I prayerfully hope we will gradually, but surely, be conformed to Christ as the Holy Spirit takes the teaching of the Word of God and applies it to our lives. "And we, who with unveiled faces all reflect the Lord's glory, are being transformed into his likeness with ever increasing glory, which comes from the Lord, who is the Spirit" (2 Corinthians 3:18).

> *My dear Redeemer and my Lord,*
> *I read my duty in thy Word;*
> *But in thy life the law appears*
> *Drawn out in living characters.*
> *Such was thy truth, and such thy zeal,*
> *Such deference to thy Father's will,*
> *Such love, and meekness so divine,*

I would transcribe and make them mine.
Be thou my pattern; make me bear
More of thy gracious image here:
Then God the Judge shall own my name
Amongst the followers of the Lamb.
— Isaac Watts

DISCUSSION QUESTIONS
WALKING IN THE FOOTSTEPS OF JESUS

1. In your own words, define the word "Christian."

2. According to 1 John 2, how important is it that a professing Christian's *claim* of being a follower of Christ be backed up with daily *conduct* to match? What does the phrase "match your conduct to your claim" mean to you?

3. Have you seen this same emphasis in your own Christian circles (church, friends, school)? What might be some dangers of assuring people of their salvation if the only criterion is their *claim*?

4. What are some character traits of Jesus that you would especially like to see better mirrored in your own life as a result of this study?

5. Spend some time praying for the Holy Spirit to work in your life specifically in those character traits that you mentioned in your answer above.

Chapter One

WHY WALK LIKE JESUS DID?

Jesus Christ has captivated the attention of millions of people over the centuries. Many of us have professed to be His followers. But, how well do we know the Jesus of the Bible? We have a great need to know this Person whom we claim as Savior and Lord. Are our lives a reflection of the character of the One whom we say we are following?

As professing Christians, we are told clearly in the Bible that we must pattern our lives after Jesus Christ. The kind of character seen in Jesus must also be seen in us. The Apostle John said it like this: "Whoever claims to live in him *must walk as Jesus did*" (1 John 2:6, emphasis added). Why should we take time to study the character traits of Jesus? Why should we be concerned with being like Jesus? A study of the New Testament reveals five reasons.

Because Christlikeness is Our Calling

Jesus stood before a Galilean crowd and said, "Come to me, all you who are weary and burdened, and I will give you rest. Take My yoke upon you and learn from me, for I am gentle and humble in heart, and you will find rest for your souls" (Matt. 11:28-30). King Jesus himself has given us His gracious command to come to Him to learn.

We are called not primarily to an institution or a particular body of doctrine, but to a real Person. It is from that real Person with all His attributes that we are to learn. King Jesus commands us to come to Him to learn, and we must obey His call. As we respond, our initiation into Christ must be followed by our imitation of Christ.

Because Christlikeness is Our Obligation

Professing that we are connected to Christ in salvation carries with it an obligation to back up that verbal claim with a lifestyle that mirrors the character of Christ. This is at the heart of John's statement, "This is how we know we are in him: whoever claims to live in him must walk as Jesus did" (1 John 2:5b-6). Faith in Jesus as Savior and conformity to His character are inseparable.

Bible commentator William Hendriksen remarked, "The apostle [Paul] never proclaimed a Christ who was a Savior but not an Example, nor a Christ who was an Example but not a Savior. Christianity for Paul was, indeed, a life, but a life based on a doctrine. And for those—for those alone!—who embrace Christ as being, by God's sovereign grace, Lord, Savior, and thus Enabler, he can also be Example."[1]

Being like Christ is a necessary standard for the Christian. Scottish theologian and pastor Sinclair Ferguson has written, "In a word, maturity equals Christlikeness. No other standard may be allowed to substitute. All other standards will be lesser, man-made alternatives that disguise the all-demanding standard God sets before us in the Scriptures."[2]

Repeatedly in the New Testament, we Christians are called upon to follow Christ in our paths to Christian maturity. In addition to 1 John 2:5b-6, consider these calls to Christlikeness:

> *I have set you an example that you should do as I have done for you* (John 13:15).
> *Your attitude should be the same as that of Christ Jesus* (Philippians 2:5).
> *Christ suffered for you, leaving you an example, that you should follow in His steps* (1 Peter 2:21).

If we are not seeking to reflect the character of Christ in our own lives, what right do we have to claim to be "Christians"?

Because Christlikeness is Our Passion

When we are drawn to Christ in salvation, we find that He becomes *precious* to us (1 Peter 2:7). *The more we get to know Him, the more we want to know Him.* Then, knowing Him more and more leads to being more like our Savior in our daily lives. After decades of being a Christian, the imprisoned missionary, Paul, could still write with passion, "I want to know Christ and the power of his resurrection and the fellowship of sharing in his sufferings, becoming like him in his death" (Philippians 3:10).

Charles H. Gabriel wrote a gospel song in the early twentieth century that is the heart-cry of every Christian. That hymn begins with this life aspiration: "More like the Master I would ever be." Theologian B. B. Warfield wrote with equal passion, "'Christ our Example,' after 'Christ our Redeemer,' no words can more deeply stir the Christian's heart than these."[3]

Because Christlikeness is our Witness

Much of what the watching world knows of Jesus Christ results from observing the lifestyles of those who claim to be united to Christ. The world's opinions of Christ largely reflect the world's opinions of Christ's followers. In 1941, New Testament scholar E. F. Harrison wrote an article on 1 Peter, commenting on the necessity for first-century Christians to model the character of Christ. In that early era, the canon of Scripture had not yet been completed and compiled. What non-believers knew of Christ, they gleaned not only from the verbal witness they heard from those who professed to be Christ's followers, but also from what they saw in the everyday lives of the Christians they knew. "It was imperative that every believer should preach with his life so as to adorn the doctrine and commend it to others."[4]

In our own day, the Bible is largely neglected. As a result we mirror the first century's lack of knowledge regarding the New Testament Scriptures. Once again, most of what the watching world knows of Christ is gained from observing the everyday lives of Christians around them. The modern Christian has a ministry of providing a "constant flesh and blood demonstration" of true Christianity.[5] On the other hand, "Nothing hinders the testimony of the Christian church more than the wide gap between our claims and our performance, between the Christ we proclaim verbally and the Christ we present visually."[6]

Because Christlikeness is our Destiny

Our lives are not purposeless. As Christians, we are heading for a destiny that God had planned for us even before He said, "Let there be light." Paul wrote of this destiny in Romans 8. Many Christians find great comfort in quoting Romans 8:28, "And we know that in all things God works for the good of those who love him, who have been called according to his purpose." Sadly, however, few believers have explored that same passage to discover what Paul was referring to as the "good" that God is working in our lives. The very next words from the pen of the Apostle Paul explain, "For those God foreknew, he also *predestined to be conformed to the likeness of his Son*" (Romans 8:29, emphasis added).

To better appreciate the significance of our God-ordained destiny, let us go back to the very beginning of the human race. God decided to make one of His creations *special*. This one creature would be placed over all other created things in order to rule them on behalf of God, the Great King. "Then God said, 'Let us make man in our image, in our likeness, and let them rule over the fish of the sea and the birds of the air, over the livestock, over all the earth, and over all the creatures that move along the ground'" (Genesis 1:26).

Adam and Eve were created *special* by God—in His own "image," in His own "likeness"—in order to represent Him and rule for Him as His *prince and princess*. Yet, the prince and princess rebelled against the Great King, desiring to be their own bosses rather than to serve as the representatives of the Sovereign. Because of their rebellion, God's likeness in man was tarnished by sin, and man's designed rule over the creation was not fulfilled.

Man's job description as God's image bearer is still in force, but unfulfilled. The author of Hebrews notes this uncompleted destiny by quoting Psalm 8, then making a candid observation: "What is man, that you are mindful of him, the son of man that you care for him? You made him a little lower than the angels; You crowned him with glory and honor and put everything under his feet" (Hebrews 2:6-8a). Then we find this sad note: "In putting everything under him, God left nothing that is not subject to him. *Yet at present we do not see everything subject to him*" (Hebrews 2:8b, emphasis added).

We might despair were it not for the encouraging words that follow, "*But we see Jesus*, who was made a little lower than the angels, now crowned with glory and honor because he suffered death, so that by the grace of God he might taste death for everyone" (Hebrews 2:9). In other words, the "first Adam" did not fulfill his obligations as God's image bearer. However, God never abandoned His goal of having man operate as His special representative, ruling this created world in the name of the Great King. When the "first Adam" failed in his mission, God set in motion His plan of redemption and restoration. He sent his own perfect Son in real human flesh as the "last Adam" (1 Corinthians 15:45) to restore what was lost by the sin of the first image bearer.

Now, as the great goal of our redemption, God is bringing all things into our lives for the "good" of making us like Christ. He is molding us and shaping us "to be conformed to the likeness of his Son." We are currently in the school of redemption, becoming more and more like Jesus. "The ultimate aim of redemption is to make every believer resemble Jesus Christ."[7] "God's whole purpose, conceived in a past eternity, being worked out for and in His people in history, to be completed in the glory to come, may be encapsulated in this single concept: *God intends to make us like Christ*" (emphasis added).[8]

Graduation day awaits us! "But we know that when he appears, we shall be like him, for we shall see him as he is" (1 John 3:2). And then, having been conformed into the image of Jesus, the "last Adam" (the very thing that was predestined for us), we shall "reign forever and ever" in His likeness and under His perfect leadership (Revelation 22:5).

If our heavenly Father has predestined us to be like Jesus, and if He is currently bringing all things into our lives to work that "good" in us, then we should be very much interested in knowing all we can about our Savior, into whose image we are being restored. Why? Because it is our destiny is to be like Jesus.

Conclusion

Why should we want to be like Jesus? There are a number of crucial reasons why we should devote our lives to knowing Jesus Christ, so that we might be more like Him. Being like Jesus is our *calling*, our *obligation*, our *passion*, our *witness*, and ultimately, our *destiny*. We must devote ourselves to the study of Christ through His holy Word, praying that His Holy Spirit would conform us to the image of our blessed Savior more and more.

May the mind of Christ my Savior
Live in me from day to day,
By His love and pow'r controlling
All I do and say.
May the love of Jesus fill me
As the waters fill the sea;
Him exalting, self abasing
This is victory.
– Kate B. Wilkinson

Notes

[1] William Hendriksen, *Exposition of Colossians and Philemon* (Grand Rapids: Baker Book House, 1964), 92.

[2] Sinclair B. Ferguson, "Being Like Jesus" in *Discipleship Journal*, 24 (November 1, 1984), p. 20.

[3] B. B. Warfield, *The Person and Work of Christ* (Philadelphia: Presbyterian and Reformed Publishing Co., 1950), p. 563.

[4] E. F. Harrison, "Exegetical Studies in 1 Peter" in *Bibliotheca Sacra*, 392 (October-December 1941), p. 459.

[5] Ibid.

[6] John Stott, *Focus on Christ* (New York: William Collins Publishers, 1979), p. 153.

[7] Leslie B. Flynn, *The Power of Christlike Living* (Grand Rapids: Zondervan, 1962), p. 13.

[8] Stott, p. 142.

DISCUSSION QUESTIONS
WHY WALK LIKE JESUS DID?

1. Name the five reasons why we should be concerned with Christlikeness.

2. Which one of these five reasons especially captures your interest? Why?

3. Briefly tell about a person who "preached with his or her life." What kind of impact did that example make on you?

4. Finish this sentence: "God intends to make us _____ — _____."

5. Thus far in your Christian experience, what does "Christian maturity" looked like to you? How do you think this picture might change through a study of Christlikeness?

6. Spend some time praying, asking God to continue His work of making you more like Jesus—no matter what that might take.

Chapter Two

WALKING IN MEEKNESS LIKE JESUS DID

What a sight it must have been! A parade of foreigners was passing through the streets of Jerusalem—Gentiles from the east. This entourage of foreign-looking, foreign-sounding men said they were looking for a *king* and were asking the local folks the way to the king's palace. What a surprise these travelers must have received when they finally arrived at the king's palace, only to find that no baby king was to be found there! Instead, these eastern "magi" were told by King Herod's advisors to look in the nearby village of Bethlehem. There, in that smaller and more humble town, they would find the King they were seeking. There they would find the young King—the King who had been born in a stable.

We are so familiar with the story of the birth of Jesus and the story of the "wise men" that we often miss a significant incongruity. We forget just how unusual it was that the *King of kings* would be born not in a king's palace, but in a stable designed for horses, donkeys, and camels. Why would the King of kings choose to make His entrance in such a humble setting?

In the previous chapter we learned of Jesus' gracious command to come "learn from Me" (Matthew 11:29). Do you remember what Jesus said about Himself in that invitation? He said, "learn from Me, for I am gentle and humble in heart." The word "gentle" in the NIV can also be translated, "humble" or "meek." We are invited—actually *commanded*—to come learn from this One who describes Himself as being *"meek and lowly in heart*" (KJV). Let us respond to this gracious command and come, learn of Christ's *meekness*.

What is "Meekness"?

An English definition of "meek" is "patient and mild; not inclined to anger or resentment; gentle or kind."[1] Some draw a slight distinction between meekness and humility. Humility is seen as an attitude or attribute a person has within himself. Meekness is *how* that humble person relates to others. In our western culture, "meekness" is sometimes understood with a negative connotation. Some assume that a meek person is powerless or weak. This distortion of the concept surely doesn't fit Jesus Christ. He characterized Himself as being meek, yet He certainly was not weak or powerless. Indeed, Jesus acknowledged that He was greater than Abraham. He demonstrated His lordship over sickness, demons, death—even sin. We must not let modern distortions determine our understanding of the biblical concept of meekness.

In the Bible, meekness is the demeanor of a person who accepts the place God has appointed for him. A meek person embraces the role God has ordained for him or her. Ultimately, we learn the meaning of meekness not from dictionaries or from popular concepts, but by observing the One who Himself is the benchmark of meekness. He is the epitome—the defining standard—the very embodiment of meekness.

Jesus was Meek in His Attitudes

Philippians 2:5-6 says, "Your attitude should be the same as that of Christ Jesus: who being in very nature God, did not consider equality with God something to be grasped." It is important to remember that Jesus Christ had existed from all eternity past as God. He had experienced all the indescribable glories of heaven (John 17:5). Yet, as He walked on this earth, He did not assert that role nor demand that glory. He never used His "God-ness" as a means of self-promotion or self-protection. Out of love for us as His people, He chose not to cling to the privileges that were rightfully His. He was willing to waive His rights in order to serve others. Jesus did not pull rank. Instead, He humbled Himself and willingly chose to "be made like His brothers in every way, in order that He might become a merciful and faithful High Priest in service to God, and that He might make atonement for the sins of the people" (Hebrews 2:17).

Jesus was Meek in His Actions

In Philippians 2:7-8 Paul wrote, "[He] made himself nothing, taking the very nature of a servant, being made in human likeness. And being found in appearance as a man, he humbled himself and became obedient to death—even death on a cross."

Jesus Stepped Down *from Heaven to Earth.*

The Prince of Glory became the Son of Man. When God the Son came to this fallen planet, He laid aside the independent use of His divine prerogatives. He who had heard the continual praise of "Holy, Holy, Holy" from the moment He had created the heavenly beings was born in a stable to the ugly sounds of donkeys and camels. He who had smelled the heavenly incense was now subject to the odors of musty straw, animal manure, and human sweat. The One who had been rich beyond measure became poor for us. "For you know the grace of our Lord Jesus Christ, that though He was rich, yet for your sakes He became poor, so that you through His poverty might become rich" (2 Corinthians 8:9). He who had been the Law-giver humbled Himself to become a Law-keeper. "But when the time had fully come, God sent His Son, born of a woman, born under law" (Galatians 4:4).

American author Les Carter challenges, "Can you grasp the enormity of this event in the manger? Only a face-to-face meeting with the Lamb in heaven will let us truly appreciate His incarnation. When we see Jesus robed in the glory that was rightfully His, we will be truly awed at His willingness to embrace humanity in this way, and we will understand that His greatness is anchored in the unlikely characteristic of humility."[2]

Jesus Stepped Down *from Glory to Humility.*

From the moment He left heaven's throne to the moment He rose from the grave, Jesus lived a life not of glory, but of humility. The Creator God walked on the very planet He personally had spoken into existence. Yet, "the world did not recognize Him. He came to that which was His own, but His own did not receive Him" (John 1: 10-11). Vainly we try to imagine the humiliation of being the King of kings, walking down a crowded road, and being recognized by no one. No one cared. Jesus lived a life of being misunderstood, of being rejected, of being persecuted.

Jesus Stepped Down *from Master to Servant.*

The King of kings became a servant of sinners. During those "silent years" from early childhood to age thirty, Jesus lived a humble life. During childhood He submitted himself to His earthly parents (Luke 2:51), even though He was their Lord. He humbled Himself to live in a home with sinful parents and half-siblings. He worked a normal "blue collar" job as a contractor building and fixing things for other people in His Nazareth neighborhood. Nobody in the village recognized Him as anything special. When He preached His first public sermon, the reaction of His neighbors was, "Isn't this Joseph's son?" (Luke 4:22). In fact, Matthew adds, "They took offense at him" (Matthew 13:57). Truly, Jesus' first thirty years were marked by meekness.

Then, during His years of public ministry, He demonstrated meekness as a lifestyle. With whom did He associate? Whom did He serve? Jesus spent time with, and ministered to, fishermen, tax-collectors, beggars, lepers, prostitutes, and Gentile foreigners. How different the meek Jesus was from the proud and pompous Pharisees, who distanced themselves from these outcasts of Jewish society! Jesus was indeed a "Friend of sinners." As He carried out His public ministry, the Bread of Life became hungry, the Water of Life became thirsty, and the Creator of the Universe had "no place to lay His head" (Matthew 8:20). Even in His supposed moment of glory on that Palm Sunday, it was said of Jesus (quoting Zechariah 9:9), "See, your King comes to you, gentle (or *meek*) and riding on a donkey" (Matthew 21:5). Truly it is said of this meek Jesus, "The Son of Man did not come to be served, but to serve, and to give his life as a ransom for many" (Matthew 20:28).

Jesus Stepped Down *from Life to Death.*

As the ultimate act of meekness, the Son of God stepped down *from life to death*. The One who was identified as "the Author of life" (Acts 3:15) voluntarily submitted to death at the hands of wicked men. The One who had life in Himself voluntarily laid aside His own life so He could die for unworthy sinners. He willingly died a painful, shameful death. "He humbled Himself and became obedient to death—even death on a cross!" (Philippians 2:8).

How Should Christ's Meekness Impact Us?

According to Philippians 2:5, our attitude "should be the same as that of Christ Jesus." Are our relationships marked by attitudes that mirror Jesus' attitude of meekness? When we consider our relationship with God, do we have a growing grasp on the reality that *"He is God, and we are not"*? Are we secure in our relationships with God through Jesus Christ? The apostle Paul showed the foundation for this attitude of Christlike meekness by these words: "If you have any encouragement from being united with Christ, if any comfort from His love, if any fellowship with the Spirit…" (Philippians 2:1). If we understand that our relationship with God the Father is based on our undeserved union with Christ, then that should produce a demeanor of meekness in our lives. There is no room for pride when we recognize that our vertical relationship with God is based entirely on grace.[3]

Likewise, our relationships with other people also should be marked by a Christlike meekness. Do we truly grasp our position in relation to other people? Do we "*in humility* consider others better than ourselves" (Philippians 2:3, emphasis added)? Or do we characteristically promote ourselves? Assert ourselves? Defend ourselves? A sure indicator that we are *not* meek is the spending of emotional energy to avoid humiliation. Meekness on our parts will contribute to the pursuit of unity in our families and in our churches. Instead of proudly promoting our own preferences and agendas, meekness should lead us to consider others better than ourselves. We can work with the other believers in our lives in "being like-minded, having the same love, being one in spirit and purpose" (Philippians 2:2).

Do our actions reflect those of Jesus, who is "meek and lowly in heart" (Matthew 11:29, KJV)? Do we do things out of "selfish ambition," or do we, in humility, pursue the interest of others? Do our lifestyles reveal Christlikeness in having a helpful attitude toward others? Are we sensitive to the welfare of others—especially our brothers and sisters in Christ? Like our meek Savior, do our lives indicate that we are willing to serve others, even if it means our own personal sacrifice?

Jesus Christ was marked by meekness in His attitudes and in His actions. He has graciously commanded us to come learn from Him—from Him who is *"meek and lowly of heart."* As we contemplate our Savior and Teacher, we will be "transformed into His [meek] likeness" (2 Corinthians 3:18). South African pastor Andrew Murray wrote, "A proud follower of the humble Jesus—this I cannot, I may not be."[4] *Lord, do your refining work. Make us more like our meek Savior.*

> *Man of Sorrows! What a name*
> *For the Son of God, who came*
> *Ruined sinners to reclaim:*
> *Hallelujah! What a Savior!*
> *Bearing shame and scoffing rude,*
> *In my place condemned he stood,*

Sealed my pardon with his blood:
Hallelujah! What a Savior!
– Philip P. Bliss

Notes:

[1] *Webster's New Twentieth Century Dictionary of the English Language, unabridged* (New York: Collins World, 1978), p. 1119.

[2] Dr. Les Carter, *Reflecting the Character of Christ* (Nashville: Thomas Nelson Publishers, 1995), p. 14.

[3] For another illustration that grasping the reality of salvation by grace alone having the effect of banishing all human pride, read 1 Corinthians 1:26-31.

[4] Andrew Murray, *Like Christ* (Philadelphia: Henry Altemus Company, n.d.), p. 173.

DISCUSSION QUESTIONS
WALKING IN MEEKNESS LIKE JESUS DID

1. Begin by prayerfully reading Philippians 2:1-11 several times.

2. How would you define the word "meek?"

3. What are some ways Jesus showed meekness in His attitudes?

4. What are some ways Jesus showed meekness in His actions?

5. How does being "meek like Jesus" relate to the popular notion of having "self-esteem?"

6. What are some ways you could show meekness to those closest to you (family, friends, fellow church members)?

7. How should the meekness of Jesus affect the corporate life of the church?

Chapter Three

WALKING WITH A MISSION LIKE JESUS DID

Jesus' Mission-Mindedness Displayed

It was a spring day in one of the most beautiful cities in the Middle East. On this particular Thursday, some sort of parade seemed to extend along the palm tree-lined streets of this oasis, known as "a little paradise." It was the week before the Passover, and many travelers were passing through the picturesque valley town of Jericho as they journeyed toward the mountaintop city of Jerusalem for the festival. Yet, one traveler seemed to be drawing most of the attention. In fact, crowds gathered along the tree-lined streets to get a glimpse of this famous man and His entourage.

The object of curiosity was a young rabbi whose unusual preaching and miracle working had gained Him a significant amount of attention. No doubt, many Jericho citizens wondered if this young rabbi and His followers would stay overnight in their beautiful city to rest before the arduous climb from the deep Jordan Valley to Jerusalem, situated in the Judean hills above them. Would the young preacher stay at the home of one of the local priests or rabbis? That would be appropriate. Preachers often stay at the home of fellow preachers when they travel.

As people jostled and shoved, trying to find a front row position for a good look at Jesus, this rabbi everyone had been talking about, an interesting scene was developing unnoticed behind them. A nicely-dressed, obviously well-to-do man was finding it difficult to get a good place from which to view Jesus and His band of followers. No one in the crowd seemed willing to let this wealthy but unpopular man pass through to the front. No one would move aside for Zacchaeus. Why should they? He had one of the most detested jobs imaginable to the Jews of Jericho. He was a tax collector. "As you would imagine, a Jew who accepted a job as a tax collector had to be motivated by sheer greed to make large sums of money and calloused to the point of complete disdain for his follow countrymen's financial plight."[1]

But this was no ordinary, run-of-the-mill tax collector. Zacchaeus was a "chief tax collector." He was in charge of the whole district around the area—one of only three "chief tax collectors" in all of Palestine. Zacchaeus was doubly unpopular with his neighbors in Jericho. Not only was he held in contempt for lining his pockets at the expense of his fellow Jews, but also he worked for those hated Gentile occupiers, the Romans. Imagine, a Jew getting rich by fleecing his fellow Jews in the name of the Roman government. No wonder no one wanted to let Zacchaeus have a front-row seat to see Jesus!

Not only was Zacchaeus wealthy and detested, but also he was short! An enterprising man, he came up with a novel solution. He climbed one of the sycamore-fig trees growing near the street. What a sight that must have been! One of the most notorious and filthy-rich citizens of Jericho was climbing a tree like a school boy.

Soon the crowds could see Jesus approaching. They craned their necks to get a better glimpse. He certainly *looked* ordinary, but the stories about Him were far from routine. Many of the common people found Him fascinating. He preached in ways they understood. He was so kind. He showed compassion to ordinary, lowly people—just like them.

The religious leaders, though, resented Jesus immensely. Rumors were spreading that something was going to happen during the Passover. Would there be a decisive confrontation between the young miracle-working rabbi from Galilee and the Jerusalem religious establishment? Who would come out on top?

As the citizens of Jericho watched and wondered, Jesus suddenly stopped under Zacchaeus's sycamore-fig tree. Cynical smiles began to spread across the faces of the watching Jews. No doubt, many in that crowd were observing this scene with joyful anticipation. Maybe this rabbi from Galilee would put the wealthy traitor, Zacchaeus, in his place. Maybe Jesus would rebuke him in front of all these people whom he had robbed. That would be great! Surely Zacchaeus was shocked when he realized that the parade had stopped directly under his tree.

But Zacchaeus was not the only one who was surprised by what happened next. The Bible tells us, "When Jesus reached the spot, he looked up and said to him, 'Zacchaeus, come down immediately. I must stay at your house today'" (Luke 19:5). What did Jesus say? Did He say that He was going to stay in the home of that *sinner*? Why would He do such a thing?

Jesus' words to Zacchaeus reveal that He was aware that their meeting was a divine appointment. Literally, Jesus said, "It is necessary for me to stay at your house today." Jesus was not merely out on a casual afternoon stroll. He was on a divine mission. He had a purpose in going to the house of this corrupt businessman. Although Zacchaeus was glad to be part of this divine appointment, the crowds were visibly and audibly displeased. "All the people saw this and began to mutter, 'He has gone to be the guest of a "sinner"'" (Luke 19:7).

But Jesus knew His mission. His divine purpose was so clear that He was not dissuaded by the disapproval of the grumbling crowd. As we follow Jesus and Zacchaeus to the tax collector's Jericho villa, we find an astonishing scene. Zacchaeus has become a changed man. He, who previously had been greedy and dishonest in his business dealings, was now humble and repentant. He volunteered, "Look, Lord! Here and now I give half my possessions to the poor, and if I have cheated anybody out of anything, I will pay back four times the amount" (Luke 19:8). How could anyone explain this amazing change? Jesus announced, "Today salvation has come to this house." The change in Zacchaeus was unexplainable in human terms. It was divinely worked. Such a change could come about only by the intervention of saving grace.

Before Jesus left Zacchaeus's home to finish His journey to Jerusalem and the crucifixion that awaited Him, He clearly declared His purpose statement—His mission. He said to the grateful Zacchaeus and to the grumbling neighbors, "For the Son of Man came to seek and to save what was lost" (Luke 19:10).

Jesus' Mission-Mindedness Declared

This was not the only time Jesus declared His mission statement. Over and over again it was said of Him and by Him that He was here on this sin-filled earth as a Man with a mission. Jesus' life was marked by *purpose*.

Even before Jesus was born in Bethlehem the angel announced that His coming would be *purposeful*. The angel said, "You are to give him the name Jesus, because he will save his people from their sins" (Matthew 1:21). Early in Jesus life He asked His mother and stepfather, "Didn't you know that I had to be in my Father's house?" (Luke 2:49). As He began His public ministry, He revealed that He was very much aware of why He was here on planet earth. "I have come to...fulfill the Law and Prophets" (Matthew 5:17, paraphrase). "My food...is to do the will of him who sent me and to finish His work" (John 4:34). Later, He explained to His men, "The Son of Man [came]... to serve, and to give his life as a ransom for many" (Matthew 20:28). In chapter 16, verse 21, Matthew observes the later part of Jesus' ministry, "From that time on Jesus began to explain to his disciples that He must go to Jerusalem." As He went through the Passion Week, He explained to His disciples, "Now my heart is troubled, and what shall I say? 'Father, save me from this hour?' No, it was for this very reason I came to this hour. Father, glorify your name!" (John 12:27-28). And as He stood before Pilate during that night-time trial, Jesus reiterated "For this reason I was born, and for this I came into the world, to testify to the truth" (John 18:37).

Jesus' clear awareness of His mission was heard in that triumphant cry from the cross, "It is finished!" (John 19:30). Mission accomplished! Jesus came to do the will of His Father. He came to seek and to save those who were lost. He came to glorify His Father's name. *And, He did it.* He completed the work the Father had given Him (John 17:4).

After Jesus went back to heaven, the Holy Spirit reminded the apostles of Jesus' mission and of His awareness of His purpose on the earth. For example, Paul would later teach, "God sent His Son…to redeem those under the Law" (Galatians 4:4-5). And the author of Hebrews wrote, "For this reason he had to be made like his brothers…in order that he might become a merciful and faithful high priest" (Hebrews 2:17).

The words of Jesus and His apostles repeatedly teach us that He was a Man on a mission. There was nothing haphazard about His life and ministry. All was done for a purpose. The very life of Jesus is marked by His mission. "I have come to do your will, O God" (Hebrews 10:7), and in doing so, He brought His Father glory (John 17:4). This purpose focused on "seeking and saving what was lost." When we look at the life and character of Jesus, we must see Him this way—as a "Man on a mission"—determined to reach the goal of glorifying the Father by doing His will.

Jesus' Mission-Mindedness Duplicated
in His Apostles

Passing the missions baton to His apostles was clearly at the forefront of Jesus' mind as He prepared for His physical departure from the earth. In praying to His heavenly Father the night before His crucifixion He prayed, "As you sent me into the world, I have sent them into the world" (John 17:18). Several days later, on the evening of resurrection day, Jesus appeared to His disciples and announced, "As the Father has sent me, I am sending you" (John 20:21). And, what were the last words of Jesus as He ascended into heaven? "But you will receive power when the Holy Spirit comes on you; and you will be my witnesses in Jerusalem, and in all Judea and Samaria, and to the ends of the earth" (Acts 1:8).

How did the mission-mindedness of Jesus Christ affect the lives and ministries of His apostles? Listen to the testimony of the Apostle Paul. He saw his life wrapped up in carrying on the mission of Jesus to bring the message of salvation to undeserving sinners. He wrote, "We are therefore Christ's ambassadors, as though God were making his appeal through us. We implore you on Christ's behalf: Be reconciled to God" (2 Corinthians 5:20). Paul couldn't stop telling people the good news of salvation in Jesus Christ. He explained the purpose of his life this way: "Yet when I preach the gospel, I cannot boast, for I am compelled to preach. Woe to me if I do not preach the gospel!" (1 Corinthians 9:16).

Jesus' Mission-Mindedness Duplicated in Us

How should we mirror our glorious, purposeful Savior? We must not meander through life, living to please ourselves with whatever captures our interest for the time being. As followers of Jesus Christ, our lives have *purpose*. We must not live meaningless, haphazard lives, but we must be *people on a mission*.

Jesus Himself gave us our life mission. His last words before going back to heaven were, "All authority in heaven and on earth has been give to me. Therefore go and make disciples of all nations, baptizing them in the name of the Father and of the Son and of the Holy Spirit, and teaching them to obey everything I have commanded you. And surely I am with you always, to the very end of the age" (Matthew 28:18-20).

The Apostle Peter explained our mission this way: "But you are a chosen people, a royal priesthood, a holy nation, a people belonging to God, *that you may declare the praises of Him* who called you out of darkness into his wonderful light" (1 Peter 2:9-10, emphasis added). Our whole lives are to be lived *purposefully* as we seek to carry out our assigned mission of telling the world about our glorious Savior.

Often, when we hear the word "missions," our minds automatically drift to thoughts of a small, select band of people who are called to take the gospel to faraway, exotic lands. While we are thankful for, and support, those missionaries sent cross-culturally, we ought not miss the everyday opportunities to carry out the mission our Lord gave us. We have the privilege of "declaring the praises of Him who called [us] out of darkness into his wonderful light" in our daily encounters with the people around us.

We can mirror the mission-mindedness of Jesus as we go to our schools and workplaces Monday through Friday. As we increasingly reflect the character of our Lord Jesus in our daily lives, the nonbelievers we see each day may have a growing curiosity. What makes us different from so many of our classmates or co-workers? The Apostle Peter counseled, "But in your hearts set apart Christ as Lord. Always be prepared to give an answer to everyone who asks you to give the reason for the hope that you have. But do this with gentleness and respect" (1 Peter 3:15).

We can mirror the mission-mindedness of Jesus as we live in our communities. Praying to have the eyes and heart of Jesus more consistently, we will begin to see the people we encounter in our neighborhoods and marketplaces as individuals who need to hear the good news about salvation in Christ alone.

Also, we begin to reflect more brightly our Lord's mission-mindedness with our still unsaved family members. With "gentleness and respect" (1 Peter 3:15), we speak warmly of our Savior, praying that He will open the eyes of our family members, even as He did ours.

O for a thousand tongues to sing
My great Redeemer's praise,
The glories of my God and King,
The triumphs of his grace.
My gracious Master and my God,
Assist me to proclaim,
To spread through all the earth abroad,
The honors of thy Name.
– Charles Wesley

Note:

[1] Dr. Les Carter, *Reflecting the Character of Christ* (Nashville: Thomas Nelson Publishers, 1995), p. 148.

DISCUSSION QUESTIONS
WALKING WITH A MISSION LIKE JESUS DID

1. From Luke 19:10, write out Jesus' mission statement.

2. Did Jesus devise His own mission statement, or was it
   assigned to Him? See Matthew 1:21 and John 17:4.

3. How sensitive was Jesus to His mission as He went
   about His life here on Earth? See Luke 2:49-50; Luke
   4:16-21; John 4:34; Matthew 16:21-23; John 19:30.

4. How did this sensitivity to His mission affect Jesus? See
   John 12:23-28; Matthew 26:36-42; John 18:36-37.

5. Is our mission statement one that we have come up with
   ourselves, or has it been assigned to us? See John 20:21 and
   Matthew 28:18-20.

6. On a slip of paper, write the names of three people you
   would like to talk to about Jesus. Use that slip of paper as
   a bookmark for your daily Bible reading, reminding you
   to pray daily for opportunities to witness to those three
   people.

Chapter Four

LIVING INCARNATIONALLY LIKE JESUS DID

He was so tired. It had been an exhausting day. He had preached multiple times that day, and now He had to deal with the pressure of the crowds of people. He climbed to the back of the boat and made a makeshift bed out of a cushion and soon fell into a deep sleep. So deep, in fact, that He didn't stir even when the boat began pitching and tossing. Water was pouring down from the sky and gushing over the gunwales of the boat. And on He slept.

The situation was becoming desperate. Soon, the wild-eyed, stressed-out disciples were shaking Jesus out of His much-needed sleep. See Him pushing the rain-soaked hair out of His eyes as He turned toward the panicked voices shouting above the storm, *"Lord, save us! We're going to drown!"*

Jesus shook off the deep sleep and crawled off His drenched cushion. Bracing Himself, He stood up in the back of that tossing boat. No doubt sounding like a frazzled dog-owner at the back door of his house in the middle of the night, Jesus shouted to the wind and waves, *"Quiet! Be still!"* Like that misbehaving dog, the wind and the waves knew the voice of their Master and immediately calmed down, becoming completely quiet at His command.

The writers of the Gospels don't tell us whether Jesus went back to sleep (I would not be surprised if He did), but they do tell us what happened to His companions. As Matthew recalls that unforgettable night, "The men were amazed and asked, 'What

kind of man is this? Even the wind and the waves obey Him?'"
(Matthew 8:27).

Indeed. *What kind of man is this?* In what category does
someone like Jesus fit? What kind of man can at one moment lie
in exhausted sleep and at the next moment command the wind
and the waves to be quiet? *What kind of man is this?* To find the
answer, we must go back to the beginning. Back not merely to
the beginning of Jesus' ministry. Not merely to the beginning of
His life here on earth. Not merely to the beginning of time. We
must go back even before that. We must sweep back the curtain
of time and peer into eternity past.

John 1:1-3 lets us take that look back before the day that God
created the universe. "In the beginning was the Word, and the
Word was with God, and the Word was God. He was with God
in the beginning. Through him all things were made; without him nothing was made that has been made." Then the
Gospel writer surprises us with, "The Word became flesh and
made his dwelling among us. We have seen his glory, the glory of
the One and Only, who came from the Father, full of grace and
truth" (John 1:14).

Did you catch that fascinating title of Jesus: "the One and
Only"? Actually, it is only one word in Greek. It means "unique."
Jesus is the only one of His kind, the only one in His category.
That's why those storm-drenched disciples were so baffled. Jesus
defied categorization. They had asked in bewilderment, "What
kind of man is this?" They were unable to place Jesus into any cat-
egory because He is the *only* One of His kind. Jesus *alone* is both
God and man. Jesus is God in the flesh. Jesus is God *incarnate*.

What Jesus Has Always Been

The Bible teaches that Jesus had always existed in eternity
past. "In the beginning was the Word" (John 1:1). Have you ever
wondered what life was like for Jesus *before* He came to the earth?
Jesus let His disciples eavesdrop as He talked to His heavenly Father the night before the cross, "And now, Father, glorify me in

your presence with *the glory I had with you before the world be-gan*" (John 17:5, emphasis added).

Jesus had always existed in eternity past "*with* God" (John 1:1, emphasis added). We can only try to imagine the eternal, perfect relationship of love between God the Father and God the Son. Jesus prayed, "for you loved me before the creation of the world" (John 17:24). No sin. No hatred. No rejection. Not even fear of rejection. Only perfect, eternal love.

Jesus had always existed in eternity past *as* God: "And the Word was God" (John 1:1). As the eternal God, Jesus had been the owner of the universe. Have you ever thought of the pre-Bethlehem Jesus as being the owner of the universe? "Every animal of the forest is mine, and the cattle on a thousand hills. I know every bird in the mountains, and the creatures of the field are mine. If I were hungry I would not tell you, for the world is mine, and all that is in it" (Ps. 50:10-12). John opens our eyes to an astonishing truth about the pre-Bethlehem Jesus. He writes that the Old Testament prophet Isaiah "saw *Jesus'* glory and spoke about *him*" (John 12:41, emphasis added). And just what was it that Isaiah saw and spoke about? Let's listen to the prophet's eyewitness account of what he saw the pre-Bethlehem Jesus to be like. "I saw the Lord seated on a throne, high and exalted, and the train of His robe filled the temple. Above him were seraphs, each with six wings: With two wings they covered their faces, with two they covered their feet, and with two they were flying. And they were calling to one another: 'Holy, holy, holy is the LORD Almighty; the whole earth is full of His glory" (Isaiah 6:1-3). What an awesome encounter Isaiah had with the pre-Bethlehem Jesus!

Jesus had also been *the Creator of the universe*: As the second person of the Trinity, He spoke into existence this whole universe by His powerful words. "For by him all things were created: things in heaven and on earth, visible and invisible, whether thrones or powers or rulers or authorities; all things were created by him and for him" (Colossians 1:16).

It's an awesome realization, isn't it? Jesus had always existed in eternity past as the Eternal One. He had always been with God.

He had always been God. He was the creator of the universe. Want a jarring experience? Read the description of Jesus as God found in John 1:1-3, then immediately drop down to verse 14. "In the beginning was the Word, and the Word was with God, and the Word was God. He was with God in the beginning. Through him all things were made; without him nothing was made that has been made…The Word became flesh and made His dwelling among us!"

What the Eternal One Became

Notice the stunning contrasts in this passage. The first contrast is that the Eternal God "became flesh" (John 1:14). The Holy Spirit could have led John to use a less bold word. He could have said, "The Word became *a human being*," but He didn't. The Holy Spirit picked a blunt word to get His point across: "The Word became *flesh*." Sometimes, if we are trying to be emphatic, we will say, *"real flesh and blood."* That is the kind of emphatic, blunt talk John is using. Jesus Christ was God-come-in-the-flesh. The Eternal God had now taken on a human body, bound by time and space. The Ancient of Days now had a body that became tired, hungry, and thirsty. God-in-the-flesh felt pain and temptation. He bled real blood and died a real death on the cross.

The second contrast is that the One who had lived in all eternity past *"with God"* had now "made His dwelling among us." Isn't it shocking to realize that the Eternal God made His entrance into this world in a smelly barn? In his book, *Knowing God,* J. I. Packer wrote, "The story is usually prettified when we tell it Christmas by Christmas, but it is really rather beastly and cruel."[1] The One who had enjoyed the perfect love of the Father "came to that which was His own, but His own did not receive Him" (John 1:11). Why was Jesus born in a barn? Because no one would give up his bed for a young lady in labor with the Son of Man. Jesus' birth was a foretaste of the life He would live on this planet. He would experience a life of rejection by the very people to whom He had given life.

The third contrast is that He who had lived for all eternity past *as God* (John 1:1) now lived the common life of a Jewish carpenter. The One who had worn the royal robes of heaven took them off and was wrapped in baby clothes. The One who had sat on the throne of the universe was laid in an animal's feeding trough. The One who had known the incense of heaven now had the odors of animal urine and manure stinging his baby nostrils. He who had known the praise of angelic beings calling "Holy, holy, holy," now heard the sounds of sheep, donkeys, and camels.

And the fourth shocking contrast: the One who had been the *Creator of the Universe* was now a dependent baby boy. The One who had spoken the universe into existence now made the soft cooing sounds of a newborn baby. The One who had sustained the universe by His divine power was now dependent on a young Jewish woman to nurse Him and change His diaper. Henry Gariepy observed in his devotional book, *100 Portraits of Christ,*

> *The Christ who walked the dusty roads of Galilee was the God who had roamed through the paths of galaxies. The Christ who lit the lakeside fire on which to cook breakfast for His tired, hungry disciples, had lit a billion stars and hung them across the midnight sky. He who asked the outcast for a drink had filled with water every river, lake, and ocean. Christ became God's self-disclosure. In Jesus, God entered humanity. Eternity invaded time.*[2]

What kind of man is this? This Man, Jesus of Nazareth, is God-come-in-the-flesh. God came and lived in our world as a real human being. Jesus is God *incarnate.*

What Does the Incarnation of Jesus Mean to You and Me?

The ultimate impact of the incarnation of Jesus Christ is that we can have eternal salvation.

Apostle Paul reminded us in 1 Timothy 1:15, "Here is a trustworthy saying that deserves full acceptance: Christ Jesus came into the world to save sinners." Had Jesus not come into our world, there would be no salvation.

But there is yet another way the incarnation of Jesus impacts our lives as His followers. The night before Jesus went to the cross to accomplish the salvation of His people, He prayed, "As you sent me into the world, I have sent them into the world" (John 17:18). And, after Jesus rose to life following His death on the cross, He announced to His disciples, "As the Father has sent me, I am sending you" (John 20:21).

As followers of the Incarnate Savior, we, too, must live incarnational lives. We cannot hide in Christian enclaves, seeking minimal contact with the world. Right from the beginning, Jesus taught His followers, "You are the light of the world. A city on a hill cannot be hidden. Neither do people light a lamp and put it under a bowl. Instead they put it on its stand, and it gives light to everyone in the house. In the same way, let your light shine before men, that they might see your good deeds and praise your Father in heaven" (Matthew 5:14-16).

The apostle Peter was on the Galilean hillside that day, hearing the Savior explain the kind of ministry His followers were to have. He later wrote, "Live such good lives among the pagans that, though they accuse you of doing wrong, they may see your good deeds and glorify God on the day he visits us" (1 Peter 2:12).

We who claim to be followers of the incarnate Lord Jesus must be infiltrating our world in order to draw people's attention to God. We must be reflecting the character of Christ in our schools, our workplaces, our neighborhoods, and our homes. We must not hide from the world. Instead, like our Savior, we must live incarnational lives for His glory.

Some of our incarnational ministries may focus on acts of mercy, of getting into the worlds of people in need. We can mirror our Savior as we befriend those who are struggling with sickness or the infirmities of old age, doing what we can to help them in their time of need. We can come alongside those who are wrestling with addictive sins, seeking firmly but lovingly to help them find their hope in Christ. We can enter the worlds of those who are socially ostracized at school or work, sitting with them in the cafeteria or break room, showing them the love of our Savior. Maybe God will call some of us to move out of our comfort zones by volunteering our time and energies to serve in a soup kitchen, a rescue mission, a thrift store, a hospice ministry, or a nursing home.

Other incarnational ministries will be directly gospel-focused. As we Christians mirror our Lord's willingness to leave the comforts of heaven and enter our fallen world, may we move out of our comfort zones to tell others of Jesus. Maybe the Lord will call us to befriend an immigrant who needs to hear the salvation story. He might move us to minister in a jail or prison. We might be led to help with Bible studies at a rescue mission.

Let's boldly pray that our Lord Jesus would give us eyes to see the opportunities He has providentially placed around us to mirror His willingness to leave His world for ours.

> *Rejoice with those who rejoice;*
> *mourn with those who mourn.*
> *Live in harmony with one another.*
> *Do not be proud,*
> *but be willing to associate with people of low position.*
> *Do not be conceited.*
> – Romans 12:15-16.

Notes:

[1] J. I. Packer, *Knowing God* (Downers Grove, IL: InterVarsity Press, 1973), p. 47.

[2] Henry Gariepy, *100 Portraits of Christ* (Colorado Springs: Victor Books, 1987), p. 35.

DISCUSSION QUESTIONS
LIVING INCARNATIONALLY LIKE JESUS DID

1. Read aloud John 1:1-14 in two different versions or paraphrases of the Bible.

2. Explore what life would have been like for Jesus before He was conceived in Mary's womb. Read Isaiah 6:1-4. Write down and discuss some of your observations concerning the sights, sounds, and smells Jesus would have experienced in heaven.

3. What comes to your mind as you contrast Jesus' earthly life with the life He had experienced before His incarnation?

4. Why did Jesus willingly come to this world "in the flesh?" Read Hebrews 2 as a catalyst for your thinking.

5. What ministries of mercy are available to you, in which you can have an incarnational ministry of coming alongside hurting people?

6. What gospel ministries are available to you that would take you out of the comfort zone of your typical lifestyle and into the "world" of other people?

7. Add to your daily prayer journal this prayer: "Lord, show me today someone whose world I should enter to show the love of Christ and share the message of Christ."

Chapter Five

WALKING IN HOLINESS LIKE JESUS DID

Ho' ly: belonging to or coming from God; hallowed; consecrated or set apart for God.[1] That seems to be the essence of "holiness"—to be dedicated to God and His purposes. A life lived in holiness is a life lived for *God's* purposes and for *God's* pleasure rather than for one's own purposes and pleasure. Conversely, a sinful life is a life lived for self–for selfish purposes and pleasures. In what way was Jesus holy? How can we be like Him–living a life of holiness? Let's visit Jesus at a very trying time in His life, and see His dedication to His heavenly Father tested, tried, and proven in holiness.

The Setting

It was very early in the public ministry of Jesus. He had just been baptized by John in the Jordan River. There Jesus had taken His stand alongside fallen man. Though He Himself was without sin, He identified with other human beings, showing Himself to be the God-Man. On the Judean banks of the Jordan River Jesus had experienced the wonderful approval of His heavenly Father. "You are my Son, whom I love; *with you I am well pleased,*" the assuring voice from heaven had said (Luke 3:22, emphasis added). There Jesus also had experienced the enabling power of the Holy Spirit who had come down on Him in visible form. What a comforting and reassuring moment that must have been for the thirty-year-old carpenter from Galilee.

Then immediately after that momentous experience, Jesus was led by the Holy Spirit into the barren, lonely Judean wilderness. What was He doing in a place like that? The wilderness was a far cry from the "paradise" that the "first Adam" had enjoyed in the Garden of Eden. The Judean wilderness was a hilly, rocky, hot, arid place. Jesus was in these barren hills by divine appointment. The Holy Spirit had led Jesus there for a specific purpose—to meet Satan head on. The Son was divinely led into the wilderness in order to have His loyalty to His Father tested and proven.

For forty days Jesus fasted. He was alone with His Father without even a bite of food to distract Him. This must have been a time of contemplating His mission on this earth, a time of communion with His loving Heavenly Father, and a time of preparation for the public ministry that lay ahead over the next three years. As Israel was forty years in the wilderness, so Jesus was forty days in the wilderness. Then Satan came.

Satan began his attack when Jesus was hungry and, no doubt, weak and tired. Satan was going to tempt Jesus, the "last Adam," in a way reminiscent of how he dealt with the "first Adam." Satan was about to do his best to destroy the dedication of Jesus to His heavenly Father—to destroy the *holiness* of Jesus. Could Satan cause this Man to abandon His dedication to His Father and lead Him to pursue instead His own purposes and pleasures? Three times Satan attacked, and three times Jesus resisted.

The Temptation to Be Selfish

The first attack is recorded in Luke 4:3. We read, "The devil said to Him, 'If you are the Son of God, tell this stone to become bread.'" Can you imagine how hungry Jesus must have been after forty days of fasting? Each of the thousands of rocks within His gaze must have reminded Him of the flat bread which He had eaten nearly every day of His thirty years on this earth. Satan attacked Jesus' loyalty to His heavenly Father by appealing to His legitimate physical appetite for food, just as he had done with Adam and Eve (Genesis 3:6) and the children of Israel (Psalm 78:18).

But Satan put a twist on this enticement by trying to get Jesus to satisfy His legitimate desire for food in an *illegitimate* way. The appeal came with the preface, "If you are the Son of God." In fact, it would be just as appropriate to translate this phrase, "*Since* you are the Son of God." Satan was saying, in effect, "Take advantage of your Sonship! Look, you're hungry. You don't have to wait for the Father to meet your needs. Maybe He won't! You have the power to satisfy yourself. Go ahead. You have the power. Use it! Satisfy yourself! Be independent! Be selfish!"

How did Jesus respond to the temptation to satisfy Himself illegitimately? He quoted Deuteronomy 8:3[2] and retorted, "It is written: 'Man does not live on bread alone.'" Now why would Jesus quote this particular verse? It seems as though Jesus was seeking to make a point to Satan by implying, "It is not really the material things that count so much in life as one's trust in and loyalty to whatever God says."

Jesus was indicating that man is more than an animal with physical appetites. He is a spiritual being in a special relationship with God Himself. Man's hope is not so much in the supply as in the *Supplier*—not so much in the gift as the *Giver*. Jesus clearly resisted Satan and maintained His holiness by giving the adversary the message, "I can trust my Father. My trust is not so much in what He provides, as it is in Him as my Father. I trust my Heavenly Father. I don't need to take things into my own hands. I will not be selfish! I will be loyal to my Heavenly Father."

The Temptation to Be Successful

Jesus had stood strong; however, Satan came at Him again, seeking to jar Jesus loose from His loyalty to His Father. In Luke 4:5-7 we find Satan showing Jesus a panorama of all the world's kingdoms. He tried to get Jesus to deny His commitment to seeking His Father's will and honor. He wanted Jesus to abandon that pursuit and instead seek His own glory. He appealed to Jesus to be "successful."

Satan implied that he himself had ownership of all the king-doms of the world. He tried to beguile Jesus with, "I will give you all their authority and splendor, for it has been given to me, and I can give it to anyone I want to" (Luke 4:6). What a usurper he is! According to Psalm 2, all the nations had been promised to the Messiah. Nevertheless, the great deceiver sought to charm Jesus, saying, in essence, "Just think, Jesus. You can have all these kingdoms without enduring the shame and pain of the cross! Wouldn't that be great? You can have the crown without the cross! Here's a shortcut!"

Such an offer surely would have been enticing. There was one little "catch," however. There was a price Jesus would have to pay if He were to accept Satan's offer. Satan said, "So, if you worship me, it will all be yours" (Luke 4:7). Satan was seeking to get Jesus to worship him instead of His heavenly Father. What a deceitful huckster Satan is. But note how Jesus responded.

Jesus once again refused to compromise His holiness—His dedication to His heavenly Father. Instead of worshiping the devil, Jesus rebuked him by referring to Deuteronomy 6:13, "Worship the Lord your God and serve Him only." What was Jesus implying? He was saying, "God *alone* is sovereign. He *alone* is worthy of our worship and service. No matter what the cost, we must worship God *alone*."

Jesus did not come to this earth to be successful in the world's eyes. He "did not come to be served, but to serve, and to give His life as a ransom for many" (Matthew 20:28). Jesus would not be duped by Satan's deceitful scheme to make Him "success-ful" by circumventing the cross. Jesus was willing to maintain His holiness—His loyalty to His heavenly Father. He was willing to follow the path laid out for Him by the Father, no matter how humbling and painful that path might be.

The Temptation to Be Spectacular

One more time Satan attacked Jesus. Jesus had remained steadfast in His loyalty to His holy Father during Satan's temptations to be selfish and to be successful. In this third temptation, Satan appealed to Jesus to be spectacular. "The devil led Him to Jerusalem and had Him stand on the highest point of the temple. 'If you are the Son of God,' he said, 'throw yourself down from here. For it is written: "He will command His angels concerning you to guard you carefully; they will lift you up in their hands, so that you will not strike your foot against a stone"'" (Luke 4:9-11).

How audacious for Satan to use God's own Word (Psalm 91:11-12) in his scheme! Do you see what Satan was attempting? In essence, he was asking Jesus, "Are you sure your heavenly Father really cares about you? Can you really trust His words of love and assurance? Maybe you ought to prove His concern. Force the hand of God the Father. Make Him prove His love and concern. Do something spectacular just to make sure He really will protect you. Jump!"

Once more Jesus demonstrated His holiness—His unswerving allegiance to His heavenly Father. Once more He rejected the appeals of the adversary by quoting from Deuteronomy. Jesus recited Deuteronomy 6:16 in its appropriate context: "Do not test the Lord your God."

When Israel was in the wilderness (even as Jesus was at this time of testing), they refused to believe God's Word. The Hebrews wanted proof that God cared. They wanted *spectacular* proof of God's concern for them. God's comment on this attitude was that the Israelites had "hard hearts." Although the Israelites (and Adam before them) failed to trust God's Word, Jesus stood strong!

We might paraphrase Jesus' response to Satan like this, "God's Word is enough. I trust Him. I don't need to put Him to the test. That is not trust. That is presumption. Demanding that God do something in addition to His already-revealed will in order to prove His love for me is a cheap shot. Real trust never resorts to tricks. The Father's revealed will is enough for me. Get out of here Satan! You won't pull me away from My heavenly Father! I will trust Him! I will be loyal to Him!"

Luke records in chapter 4, verse 13, "When the devil had finished all this tempting, he left Him until an opportune time."

Our Own Holiness

How does this story of the holiness of Jesus affect you and me? First, it reminds us of the *great hope* we have in Jesus—our victorious leader! Even though the first Adam failed the test in the Garden of Eden, and even though Israel failed the test in the wilderness, Jesus passed with flying colors! His holiness—His dedication to His Father's priorities and pleasure—remained unmoved and untarnished in this encounter with the enemy. The first Adam failed. The last Adam conquered! Jesus is the One who "has been tempted in every way, just as we are—yet was without sin" (Hebrews 4:15).

As believers, *we too can know victory*. "In all these things we are more than conquerors through Him who loved us" (Romans 8:37). As people who are in Christ, we are no longer under the bondage of sin. Satan has no claims on us. We are free to refuse to yield to Satan's evil schemes. "He has rescued us from the dominion of darkness and brought us into the kingdom of the Son" (Colossians 1:13).

Second, in this true story Jesus *serves as the supreme example of holiness*. In John 5:30, Jesus explained, "I seek not to please myself, but him who sent me." As believers, we are under obligation *"to walk as Jesus did."* Just as our Lord did in the Judean wilderness, we too can, and should, resist the subtle schemes of Satan. We also have been called to be sons and daughters of God. We must walk worthy of the calling we have received (Ephesians 4:1), living a life of obedient loyalty to the Father who called us.

Satan will tempt us even as he did Adam, the Israelites, and Jesus, to be "selfish," "successful," and "spectacular." Following the example of Jesus, we, too, must resist Satan's schemes by relying on God's Word. Like Jesus, we must have an unswerving loyalty to the priorities, purpose, and pleasure of our heavenly Father. Like Jesus, doing the will of our Father should be our delight

(John 4:34). We must be willing to use God's Word as a sword in our hands when we are in battle with our archenemy. Satan is both subtle and bold. Yet, as children of God, walking in the Spirit, with the Sword of God's Word in our hands, "we are more than conquerors through Him who loved us" (Romans 8:37).

> *And though this world with devils filled,*
> *Should threaten to undo us,*
> *We will not fear for God hath willed,*
> *His truth to triumph through us.*
>
> *The prince of darkness grim,*
> *We tremble not for him;*
> *His rage we can endure,*
> *For lo! His doom is sure;*
> *One little word shall fell him.*
> – Martin Luther

Notes:

[1] *Webster's New Twentieth Century Dictionary of the English Language, unabridged* (New York: Collins World, 1978), p. 868.

[2] As Dr. Don Garlington has noted in his excellent booklet, *Jesus the Unique Son of God: Tested and Faithful,* "Since Deuteronomy particularly focuses on the testing factor, it is natural enough that the replies of Jesus to Satan are all derived from this book" (page 13). This booklet is recommended to gain a more complete understanding of the testing of Jesus in the wilderness. It can be acquired from Canadian Christian Publications, 30 Harding Blvd. W., Suite 612, Richmond Hill, Ontario, Canada L4C 9M3.

DISCUSSION QUESTIONS
WALKING IN HOLINESS LIKE JESUS DID

1. In your own words, what is the essence of "holiness"?

2. What might be some examples in everyday life of how Satan tempts believers to abandon their loyalty to God in order to be "selfish?" "successful?" "spectacular"?

3. When might Christians be most vulnerable to the attacks of Satan?

4. How does Jesus' victory over Satan impact the way you respond to temptations?

5. With what truths should we arm ourselves as followers of Jesus in order to withstand the seductions of Satan? To prompt your thinking, read these passages: Romans 6:11-14; Ephesians 6:10-18; James 4:7; 1 Peter 5:8-9.

6. What hope is there when we *have* yielded to Satan's temptations? See Proverbs 28:13 and 1 John 1:9. In your quiet time with God, read Psalm 32 and Psalm 51. Talk to God about your desire to be forgiven and to live a life of holiness.

7. How can we help one another in the body of Christ in our resistance against Satan's subtle schemes to seduce believers? See Ephesians 6:18 and Hebrews 3:12-14.

Chapter Six

ACCEPTING OTHERS LIKE JESUS DID

Diversity among the Apostles

Have you ever considered how much diversity there was among the twelve men Jesus chose to be His apostles? Darrell Bock, professor of New Testament studies at Dallas Theological Seminary, has observed, "Jesus' choosing of the Twelve reflects a unique, diverse group. He did not select a homogeneous club."

Jesus chose men who represented a variety of personality types. Peter, for example, strikes us as a true extrovert, always ready to speak his mind, always ready to act. His brother, Andrew, however, seems to be an introvert, quiet and reserved. Jesus also selected men from opposite ends of the political spectrum. He chose Simon the Zealot to join His band of followers. The nickname "Zealot" reveals that this Simon would have been a rabid Jewish patriot, passionately opposing the Roman occupiers. We have to wonder what kind of discussions Simon had with Matthew as they sat around the campfire in the evenings. Matthew had been a tax-collector before he met Jesus. He had actually collaborated with the Roman government in his despised but lucrative occupation.

Jesus' band of apostles was not a haphazard collection of volunteers. Jesus chose them. The night before Jesus died on the cross, He reminded this diverse group, "You did not choose me, but I chose you" (John 15:16). Jesus accepted extroverts as well as introverts. He accepted political "conservatives," and He accepted political "liberals." The unifying factor was not similar personality types or political persuasions. The unifying factor was Jesus Himself.[2]

Diversity in Our Churches

How diverse is the congregation in your local church? Intermingled in the typical church in our western culture are people of various races, ethnic backgrounds, educational levels, vocations, marital statuses, ages, and residential communities. Added to these differences are the dissimilar salvation histories of the various church members. Some were saved as children and grew up in Christian homes. Some were saved as teens or college students, and still others were saved when older, out of lifestyles of shameful worldliness. Now to add even more to the diversity, people in the church hold different convictions and preferences regarding style of music, style of dress, and Bible translations!

Yet, all the members of the church profess to believe in and follow the same Lord. We all profess to be part of *one* body of believers. How can this work? How can such a diverse group of people ever live and function with peace and unity? How can such a varied collection of individuals ever function as a cohesive body of believers? How can a church work together in promoting the cause of Christ in its own community and generation? Is it any wonder that some churches experience painful church splits? Has *your* church faced this challenge? Our churches today are not the first to face this daunting reality.

Diversity in a New Testament Church

In Paul's day, the church in Rome—a church made up of people with very different backgrounds and convictions—struggled with this issue of unity and acceptance. What were the potentially divisive issues in Rome? What were the differences that made a mutual acceptance of one another in this local church so difficult to achieve? In Romans 14 and 15, the apostle describes two noticeably different camps or groups within that one local body of believers. In Romans 14:2 Paul writes, "One man's faith allows him to eat everything, but another man, whose faith is weak, eats only vegetables." Then in Romans 14:5 he explains, "One man considers one day more sacred than another; another man considers every day alike." So, the differences this church wrestled with centered on differing convictions regarding *diet* and *days.*

Camp One: the Conservatives

One noticeable camp in the church had strong convictions about *not* eating certain types of food and *not* doing certain things on designated days. Paul referred to the people in this group as those whose "faith is weak." This group most likely was made up of people with Jewish backgrounds. These believers were having trouble trusting the sufficiency of Christ's fulfillment of the Old Covenant. They thought it necessary to bolster the work of Christ with the observance of certain Old Covenant laws. They were having difficulty letting go of their Old Covenant practices such as dietary restrictions and observances of the Sabbath and other holy days.

Camp Two: the Progressives

The other identifiable camp in the local church had strong convictions regarding their *liberty* to eat any kind of food and to do a variety of things on any given day of the week. Their confidence in the sufficiency of Christ's ministry of fulfilling the Law was strong. Most likely this group was made up primarily of people with Gentile backgrounds. However, some Christians with Jewish backgrounds were also in this group. Paul was an ethnic Jew (even being trained as a Pharisee), but counted himself in this latter group (Romans 15:1). In Romans 14:14 the apostle asserted emphatically, "As one who is in the Lord Jesus, I am fully convinced that no food is unclean in itself." Paul referred to this group, to which he belonged, as being the "stronger brothers."

What the Two Groups Had in Common

These two very different groups had some things in common. Both groups were made up of genuine believers who sincerely desired to please God (Romans 14:3, 13). In Romans 14:6 Paul explains, "He who regards one day as special, does so to the Lord. He who eats meat, eats to the Lord, for he gives thanks to God; and he who abstains, does so to the Lord and gives thanks to God." Another commonality that Paul mentioned repeatedly is that all believers in both camps will give an account to God Himself for their lives (Romans 14:4 and 10-12).

There is something else that was common to both of these differing groups at Rome. Both were critical of those who were different. The two groups despised each other, holding the others at a distance except to debate. The *weaker* Christians were looking down their noses at the *stronger* Christians. One can almost imagine the weaker brothers whispering, "bunch of liberals," under their breath, making sure they kept their distance.

Equally guilty, the *stronger* Christians were being critical of their weaker brothers and sisters. It doesn't stretch the imagination too much to hear these church members muttering among themselves about those "legalists" in the church with their stringent scruples concerning diet and days. Maybe they were harping about those "immature Christians" who needed to "get with it." Apparently, relational boundaries were being erected by people on both sides of these issues. No doubt they expressed attitudes such as "Why should I be his friend? I know I'm right, and he's wrong!"

Paul's Counsel to Diverse Churches:
Accept One Another

So, what counsel did the apostle Paul give to this divided church? First he wrote, "The man who eats everything must not look down on him who does not, and the man who does not eat everything must not condemn the man who does, for God has accepted him" (Romans 14:3). He also exhorted, "Let us stop passing judgment on one another" (Romans 14:13).

Paul made it clear that not everyone would agree on these "disputable matters" (Romans 14:1). In this extended passage the apostle never said the two groups must ultimately "agree" with each other. He never asked one group to abandon its convictions (though he makes no secret of his own view on these matters regarding "diet and days"). He didn't call for a compromise position somewhere in the middle. But he *did* call for the church to stop the criticism and judgment.

The responsibility to judge lies with God Himself. Christians should not seek to take over God's role in judging other Christians' convictions on matters of diet and days. "You, then, why do you judge your brother? Or why do you look down on your brother? For we will all stand before God's judgment seat" (Romans 14:10). Christians must not erect barriers that Jesus, the head of the church, never erected.

Instead of spending time and energy seeking to judge the Christian who is different, the church member is to spend his time and energy on what will promote peace and Christian growth in the church. In Romans 14:19, Paul challenges every church member, "Let us therefore make every effort to do what leads to peace and mutual edification." Instead of spending energy trying to promote "my side" or show the people on the "other side" just how wrong they really are, the Christian must do his thoughtful best to ask, "Will this attitude, comment, or action promote the unity of our local body? Will this promote the spiritual growth of my brothers and sisters in Christ?" Our goal should not be to "please ourselves," but to deal patiently with our differing brothers in a way that will build them up spiritually. This is especially true if one considers himself to be one of the "stronger" ones (Romans 15:1-2).

An encouraging and revealing word from the apostle in this passage gives a significant clue as to how people in local churches with such differing convictions can live in peace and harmony. Paul offers this blessing upon the church, "May the God who gives endurance and encouragement give you a spirit of unity among yourselves *as you follow Christ Jesus,* so that with one heart and mouth you may glorify the God and Father of our Lord Jesus Christ" (Romans 15:5-6, emphasis added). Believers in both camps were assumed to be following Christ Jesus.

And what did that following of Jesus entail in this situation? "Accept one another, then, *just as Christ accepted you*, in order to bring praise to God" (Romans 15:7, emphasis added). The word "accept" is a command "to take another to yourself in an embrace," or "to take someone into friendship." The concept is not mere toleration, but a genuine embracing of the other as a friend and brother in Christ.

Jesus is Our Motivation for Accepting One Another

Jesus is the *motivation* for us to accept our fellow Christians who differ with us on these matters. When we think about the work of Christ, we realize that *He* has accepted all kinds of people into His kingdom. He has accepted Jew and Gentile, slave and free, male and female, rich and poor, young and old, people from morally upright backgrounds and people from decadent lifestyles. All these very different people were brought into the kingdom by the same Savior, shedding the same blood, and extending the same grace. They were no more acceptable than we were when Christ accepted us.

When we think of what it cost our precious Savior to accept that differing brother or sister of ours, we need to pause and reflect: look what it cost Jesus to accept him or her. How can we treat His acceptance of others so lightly? How dare we communicate through our words and demeanor, "Well, maybe *Jesus* accepted that person, *but we're sure not going to!*" What audacity to reject someone who was accepted by Jesus at the cost of His own precious blood! "Do not by your eating destroy your brother for whom Christ died" (Romans 14:15). "Do not destroy the work of God for the sake of food" (Romans 14:20).

Jesus is Our Model for Accepting One Another

Jesus is also our *model* in accepting others. Paul wrote, "Accept one another, then, just as Christ accepted you" (Romans 15:7). We must reflect on the life of our Savior whom we are following. He never sought to please Himself. Instead, out of love for others, He was willing to take the insults that other people deserved (Romans 15:3). Like our Lord, we are to "die to self"—our own preferences—and out of a loving concern for our brother who is different from us, we are to reach out humbly with open arms and draw him close to ourselves.

Our Lord drew to Himself people who were considered by many to be unacceptable. Into His circle of followers He called tax collectors, women and children, prostitutes, and even some Pharisees. He even accepted the likes of you and me! Christ's kingdom has such breadth, considering the variety of races, ethnic backgrounds, social and economic statuses, and ages of people for whom He died.

Following His example, we, too, must accept believers who are from a variety of backgrounds, preferences, and convictions. If we claim to be true Christians, then we *"must walk as Jesus did"* (1 John 2:6) by accepting other Christians who do not share all our convictions on these matters. Accepting others might not be *comfortable* and might not be *popular*. It certainly wasn't for Jesus when He accepted these people. Should we do any less?

The Benefit of Accepting One Another

What should be the wonderful result if we indeed follow the example of our Lord in "accepting others?" Paul writes that doing this is "in order to bring praise to God" (Romans 15:7). He goes on to explain that God *deliberately* chose to put His glory on display by saving people from all kinds of backgrounds and forming them into "one new man."

Jesus Christ came and ministered His grace to both Jews and Gentiles. This was always part of His plan. "His *purpose* was to create in Himself one new man out of the two, thus making peace, and in this one body to reconcile both of them to God through the cross, by which He put to death their hostility" (Ephesians 2:15-16, emphasis added). "His *intent* was that now, through the church, the manifold wisdom of God should be made known to the rulers and authorities in the heavenly realms, according to His eternal *purpose* which he accomplished in Christ Jesus our Lord" (Ephesians 3:10-11, emphasis added).

God deliberately saves people of diverse backgrounds, so that He can put His own glorious power and wisdom on display. He wants everyone to be impressed by how He can form one new "man" out of people of diverse backgrounds. Accomplishing this in the church brings Him praise and glory. When we choose to exclude from fellowship those whom Christ has chosen to include, we are undermining His goal of displaying His glory in His church.

So, Jesus chose to accept undeserving sinners of differing stripes, so that He could bring praise to His Father. He is making something entirely *new*. He wants everyone to be impressed with His wisdom and ability to bring diverse people together. Why then would we choose to run counter to His purposes by excluding from fellowship brothers and sisters in Christ who happen to have convictions that differ from ours on these "disputable matters?" We must accept our brothers and sisters "in order to bring praise to God," "so that with one heart and mouth you may glorify the God and Father of our Lord Jesus Christ" (Romans 15:7 & 6). The church should be filled with people who don't necessarily see all the details the same, but who nevertheless *accept one another* just as Christ has accepted them to the praise of God the Father.

Now to Him who is able to do immeasurably more
than all we ask or imagine,
according to His power that is at work within us,
to Him be glory in the church
and in Christ Jesus

throughout all generations,
for ever and ever! Amen.
– Ephesians 3:20-21.

Notes:

[1] Darrell L. Bock, *The NIV Application Commentary: Luke* (Grand Rapids: Zondervan, 1996),
p. 181.

[2] For more on Jesus as the unifying factor, see John 17:20-23.

DISCUSSION QUESTIONS
ACCEPTING OTHERS LIKE JESUS DID

1. Read Romans 14:1 through 15:7. What were some of the differences facing the church in Rome?

2. Name some of the diversities you have noticed in your own church.

3. What might be some "disputable matters" facing churches in our day and culture?

4. In what ways does focusing on Christ's acceptance of us impact our readiness to accept those Christians who differ from us?

5. How is the unity (or disunity) in your own church impacting the corporate testimony your church has in your community? Read John 17:20-23; Ephesians 2:15-16; Ephesians 3:10-11 before discussing the answer to this question.

6. What might be your responsibility in improving the unity of your church? (For example, is there someone "different" in the church whom you should befriend? In what ways can you take the initiative in reaching across the barriers that keep people apart?)

7. Write out a prayer for your church using the thoughts of Romans 15:5-7.

Chapter Seven

HAVING COMPASSION LIKE JESUS DID

Stories about Jesus were finding their way to John the Baptist even in prison. There, in Herod's fortress prison of Machaerus east of the Dead Sea, he had been told stories of what Jesus had been doing. In John's mind an incongruity seemed to exist between the Messiah he had been announcing and this Jesus who had been preaching and doing miracles in Galilee.

The Messiah John the Baptist had been describing in his prophetic announcements was one of wrath and judgment. John had unapologetically and passionately proclaimed to the crowds who had made the effort to venture into the Jordanian desert, "…one more powerful than I will come, the thongs of whose sandals I am not worthy to untie. He will baptize you with the Holy Spirit and with fire. His winnowing fork is in his hand to clear his threshing floor and to gather the wheat into his barn, but he will burn up the chaff with unquenchable fire"(Luke 3:16-17).

Incredibly, though, this Jesus of Nazareth had been going about Galilee not clearing the spiritual threshing floor nor burning up chaff with unquenchable fire. He was healing sick people and preaching a gospel of salvation! As Frederick Bruner honestly observed:

> *Jesus has not yet attacked any of the reigning political or economic powers; in his miracles he has simply picked up the pieces left by evil forces. Today, Jesus' work would be derisively called "an*

*ambulance ministry," picking up the crushed
victims of evil structures but failing to combat
those evil structures themselves… Jesus is out in the
provinces healing sick, insignificant little individuals
here and there, but not doing anything to change
the basic structural problems in Israel's life…
The whole rotten religio-ideological system seems
thoroughly unthreatened by Jesus' do-goodism in
the hills. What is more, John is in prison, and Herod
(the embodiment of the oppressive Establishment)
is still on the throne and about to have John's head.
What kind of Messiah is this…?*[1]

John wanted clarification of this apparent discrepancy. So, he
sent two of his own pupils on the long journey north to Galilee
to ask Jesus this one crucial question, "Are *you* the one who was
to come, or should we expect someone else?" (Matthew 11:3,
emphasis added).

The reply Jesus gave was clear, even if surprising, to John the
Baptist and his disciples. It revealed Jesus to be the compassionate Messiah. Alluding to the prophecies of God through Isaiah
(Isaiah 35:5-6 and 61:1), Jesus answered their query, "Go back
and report to John what you hear and see: *The blind receive sight,
the lame walk, those who have leprosy are cured, the deaf hear, the
dead are raised, and the good news is preached to the poor.* Blessed
is the man who does not fall away on account of me" (Matthew
11:4-6, emphasis added).

Jesus Was *Identified* by Compassion

John the Baptist had not been wrong in his descriptions of
the coming Messiah, but he was unaware that the ministries
of wrath and judgment would be carried out primarily at the
Messiah's *second* coming. Jesus was assuring John that He was
indeed the Messiah. And on what did the credentials of the
Messiah primarily focus? The character of the Messiah at His

first coming focused largely on *compassion*. Jesus the Messiah was *identified* by compassion. Jesus was clearly explaining to John that marks of *compassion* were what identified Him as the Messiah. That had been prophesied through God's spokesman, Isaiah. And now, here was the fulfillment in Jesus of Nazareth, God's promised Messiah.

Jesus *Illustrated* Compassion

As we study the Gospels, we see clearly that Jesus the Messiah was indeed characterized by compassion. In fact, "No feature of our Lord's earthly career is more conspicuous, or more likely to arrest every reader of His life, than the tenderness of His feeling for the woes and suffering of men."[2] Jesus truly cared for people, and He showed it. Jesus obviously was affected by people with real needs, and He reached out to those people with His mercy. Andrew Murray observed, "His whole life was a manifestation of the compassion with which He had looked on the sinner from everlasting, and of the tenderness with which He was moved at the sight of misery and sorrow. He was in this the true reflection of our compassionate God."[3] Let's explore various kinds of people to whom Jesus showed compassion.

Jesus showed compassion for people who were *hurting*. Many who had *physical* hurts were touched by His compassion. For example, the Gospels tell the story of two blind beggars who cried out to Jesus, "Lord, Son of David, have mercy on us" (Matthew 20:31). Even though the crowd tried to hush them, Jesus heard their plea. When He asked them "What do you want me to do for you?" they replied, "Lord, we want our sight." Matthew relates, "Jesus had *compassion* on them and touched their eyes. Immediately they received their sight and followed Him" (Matthew 20:32-34, emphasis added).

Jesus also had compassion for people who were hurting from *grief*. Consider the character of Jesus as He approached the gate of the Galilean town of Nain. As His happy procession of followers was about to enter the town, they met a sad procession making its way out toward the town cemetery. Following the coffin was a woman who had the multiple grief of being a widow and now burying her son—her only son.

Luke records in chapter 7, verses 12-13, "As he [Jesus] approached the town gate, a dead person was being carried out— the only son of his mother, and she was a widow. And a large crowd from the town was with her. When the Lord saw her, *his heart went out to her* and he said, 'Don't cry'" (emphasis added). Do we see the genuine compassion of our Savior? "His heart went out" to this grieving, widowed mother. What a comfort it is to us when our hearts are broken with the grief of losing loved ones. Our Savior cares.

Jesus also had compassion for *people whom society rejected.* Tax collectors were some of the most unwelcome people in Jewish society, yet Jesus went against the grain of acceptable religious practice and reached out to the ostracized tax collectors. Matthew recalled that exciting evening when he had a dinner at his own home for his old friends and his new master. The religious establishment could not believe that Jesus would associate with such pariahs of Jewish society. The Pharisees asked Jesus' disciples, "Why does your teacher eat with tax collectors and 'sinners'?" Jesus responded to their critical question by calling attention to His own heart of compassionate mercy. He retorted, "It is not the healthy who need a doctor, but the sick. But go and learn what this means: 'I desire mercy, not sacrifice.' For I have not come to call the righteous, but sinners" (Matthew 9:11-13).

Others who lived with the pain of rejection also experienced the unexpected compassion of Jesus personally. Among them were prostitutes (Luke 9:36-50), children (Mark 10:13-16), and lepers (Mark 1:40-45). Regarding lepers–the "AIDS patients" of that day, Mark recorded a beautiful picture of our Lord. In Mark 1:40-41 we read, "A man with leprosy came to him and begged him on his knees, 'If you are willing, you can make me clean.' *Filled with compassion*, Jesus reached out his hand and touched the man. 'I am willing,' he said. 'Be clean!'" (emphasis added).

What compassion Jesus had on these people who were forced to live on the very fringes of society, cut off from normal loving relationships. Jesus was "filled with compassion" toward this leper whom everyone else avoided. Jesus touched him. Jesus healed him. Jesus showed *compassion*.

Jesus had compassion especially for those who were *spiritually lost*. There were times when Jesus would look at large crowds of people who were on their way to hell, and His heart would break. Matthew recalls, "When he saw the crowds, he had compassion on them, because they were harassed and helpless, like sheep without a shepherd" (Matthew 9:36). Jesus taught His disciples to pray to the Lord of the harvest to raise up workers who would reach these lost sheep (Matthew 9:35-38; also see Matthew 23:37).

Jesus cared deeply about lost people. Take note of how Jesus dealt with the "rich young ruler." Mark related that "Jesus looked at him and loved him" (Mark 10:21). Truly, Jesus had compassion on people who were spiritually lost—whether an upright, religious young man or a woman who had earned a bad reputation with her sin (John 4:7-42).

John the Baptist had good reason to be reassured. Jesus was indeed the Messiah. His *compassion* marked him as the Messiah. His very life and ministry were living illustrations of Messiah-like compassion. His heart went out to people who were suffering physically, people who were grieving with the loss of loved ones, people who were rejected by their families and neighbors, and people who were spiritually lost.

His compassion cost Him. It cost Him His *energy*. He spent long, exhausting days helping hurting people by healing them and by telling them the good news. It cost Him His *reputation*. He was slurred with the epithet, "friend of sinners." Finally, His compassion cost Him His *life*. The ultimate act of compassion was His death on that Roman cross. He *voluntarily* gave up His own life for ill-deserving sinners. Yes, tell John this, "The blind receive sight, the lame walk, those who have leprosy are cured, the deaf hear, the dead are raised, and the good news is preached to the poor" (Matthew 11:5). Tell the world this: *Jesus is the compassionate Messiah.*

Our Compassion

Are we, as people who have been rescued by the saving compassion of Jesus the Messiah, living lives marked by *compassion*? Andrew Murray observed, "What abundant occasion is there every day for the practice of this heavenly virtue, and what a need of it in a world so full of misery and sin! Every Christian ought therefore by prayer and practice to cultivate a compassionate heart, as one of the most precious marks of likeness to the blessed Master."[4]

Can we with integrity echo the words of the Apostle Paul, "How I long for all of you with the affection (literally, "compassion") of Christ Jesus" (Philippians 1:8)? Is the compassion of Christ flowing through us when we see hurting people? Grieving people? Rejected people? Lost people? Like our compassionate Messiah, are we willing to sacrifice our energy, our resources, our reputations, our lives for the benefit of others?

The Lord confronted me with my own pride and lack of compassion as I stood in public view, waiting to be seated at the restaurant. Earlier that morning I had stopped by the sparse and filthy apartment of an alcoholic man with whom several of us in the church had been sharing the gospel. I had spotted a half-empty bottle of malt liquor on his dirty table and asked, "Mike, is that what you've had for breakfast?" When he nodded sheepishly, I said, "Come on. Let's get you a real breakfast."

I lost my own appetite on the short trip to the restaurant. On the way, I had to pull off to the side of the road as Mike lost the malt liquor rebelling in his otherwise empty stomach. Now, there we were, Mike and I, waiting to be seated while standing in full view of a room full of fellow diners. The few minutes we waited seemed to crawl by as I began to wonder what the watching diners were thinking. Mike was disheveled, unshaven, dirty–even smelly. Standing beside him, I began to be concerned about my own reputation. We live in a small town. People recognize one another. I'm a pastor. I've got a reputation to uphold. What will people think of me standing with such a loser?

Then the Holy Spirit rebuked me, even as I stood uncomfortably next to Mike. A flood of shame flowed over my conscience as the Spirit reminded me, "Jesus was not ashamed to call you His brother.[5] He showed compassion on you by coming to this earth to save you, sacrificing everything—His reputation, even His life. Are you not willing, Larry, to sacrifice your own reputation to show Christ's compassion to this alcoholic?" "Forgive me, Lord," I prayed in my heart as the waitress finally seated my friend and me.

"We who owe everything to His compassion, who profess ourselves His followers, who walk in His footsteps and bear His image, oh, let us exhibit His compassion to the world. We can do it. He lives in us. His Spirit works in us. Let us with much prayer and firm faith look to His example as the sure promise of what we can be."[6]

> *When the Son of Man comes…the King will say to those on his right, "Come, you who are blessed by my Father; take your inheritance, the kingdom prepared for you since the creation of the world. For I was hungry and you gave me something to eat, I was thirsty and you gave me something to drink, I was a stranger and you invited me in, I needed clothes and you clothed me, I was sick and you looked after me, I was in prison and you came to visit me."*
>
> *Then the righteous will answer him, "Lord, when did we see you hungry and feed you, or thirsty and give you something to drink? When did we see you a stranger and invite you in, or needing clothes and clothe you? When did we see you sick or in prison and go to visit you?" The King will reply, "I tell you the truth, whatever you did for one of*

the least of these brothers of mine, you did for me"
(Matthew 25:31-40, emphasis added).

O to be like Thee! Full of compassion,
Loving, forgiving, tender and kind,
Helping the helpless, Cheering the fainting,
Seeking the wandering sinner to find.
Oh, to be like Thee! Oh, to be like Thee,
blessed Redeemer, pure as Thou art!
Come in Thy sweetness, Come in Thy fullness;
Stamp Thine own image deep on my heart.
– Thomas O. Chisholm

Notes:

[1] Frederick Dale Bruner, *Matthew, Volume 1* (Dallas: Word, 1987), p. 409.

[2] William Garden Blaikie, *The Inner Life of Christ* (Minneapolis, MN: Klock & Klock, 1982 reprint), p. 120.

[3] Andrew Murray, *Like Christ* (Philadelphia: Henry Altemus Co., n. d.), p. 104.

[4] Murray, pp. 106-107.

[5] The passage that came to my mind was Hebrews 2:11, "So Jesus is not ashamed to call them brothers."

[6] Murray, p. 109.

DISCUSSION QUESTIONS
HAVING COMPASSION LIKE JESUS DID

1. What is one of your favorite stories in the Bible that describes Jesus showing compassion? Why does that story grip you?

2. What did the compassion of Jesus cost Him?

3. Relate the story of someone showing compassion to you during a difficult time in your life.

4. What are some ideas for ministries of compassionate mercy that your church might become involved in?

5. What are some ideas for ministries of gospel compassion (evangelistic) that your church might become involved in?

6. Who (or what kind of people) is God placing on your heart to whom you can show the compassion of Jesus?

7. Read aloud Matthew 25:31-40. Let that passage now prime your heart as you ask God to give you a heart and life marked with compassion as you continue to walk as Jesus did.

Chapter Eight

SUFFERING LIKE JESUS DID

"He was despised and rejected by men, a man of sorrows, and *familiar with suffering*" (Isaiah 53:3, emphasis added). Those prophetic words were spoken about the Messiah by the prophet Isaiah 700 years before Jesus Christ was born in that Bethlehem stable. Did this prophecy prove to be true? Oh, yes. Jesus was indeed very *"familiar with suffering"* during His thirty-three years on this fallen world.

Jesus Experienced Physical Suffering

He knew *physical* suffering of various kinds. During His 40 days of temptation in the wilderness, Jesus experienced hunger and thirst. He knew the bone-aching exhaustion that came from long hard days of ministering to people. And, He drank fully from the cup of suffering found in the diabolical form of execution we know as crucifixion.

Jesus Experienced the Suffering of Rejection

Jesus also knew the pain of *rejection*. He knew quite personally the suffering that comes from being rejected. In fact, the Apostle John, who was one of Jesus' closest companions, noted this painful reality when he wrote, "He came to that which was His own, but His own did not receive Him" (John 1:11). Although Jesus experienced a brief period of popularity, the time came when "many of His disciples turned back and no longer followed Him" (John 6:66). This painful rejection culminated on that afternoon when midnight fell. As Jesus looked down from the cross, He saw from among His many previous followers only young John and a handful of women. Then, the ultimate pain of rejection came as Jesus cried out, "My God, my God, why have You forsaken me?" (Matthew 27:46).

Jesus Experienced Spiritual Suffering

Jesus also experienced a kind of *spiritual* suffering unknown to you and me. He was sinless, yet He had to live day in and day out in a world polluted by sin. He had lived in a sinless, curse-free heaven before coming to this earth. How He must have suffered deep in His soul to see and feel the effects of sin and its curse all around Him as He went through daily life. And ultimately, He bore a kind of suffering that is unspeakable and inexplicable to us fallen people. Jesus, the One who knew no sin, actually *became* sin for us (2 Corinthians 5:21). What anguish did the Sinless One feel in having His pure soul and body carry the dreadful weight of the sin of all His people? Contrary to the expectations that most people had in looking for the Messiah, Jesus was marked by being "despised and rejected by men, a man of sorrows and *familiar with suffering*"(Isaiah 53:3, emphasis added).

How Jesus *Could* Have Responded to Suffering

What must capture our interest is the answer to this important question, "How did Jesus *respond* to suffering?" Did our Savior use His divine prerogative and *strike back* at those who hurt Him? No. Well then, did Jesus have some kind of *spiritual anesthetic* that kept Him from feeling the pain of suffering? No. In fact, being sinless, His senses and His emotions would have been *perfect*. Jesus would have felt the various kinds of sufferings *perfectly*. No sin dulled His feelings. No calluses encased His heart.

Understanding *how Jesus responded* to suffering and following in His steps will revolutionize how we Christians live our lives in this fallen, painful world. Like our Savior (though, no doubt, to a lesser degree), we believers also are familiar with suffering. We live in a world that has been infiltrated by sin and dominated by the curse. We suffer physically, relationally, and spiritually. How are we supposed to *take* suffering? Should we live by that bumper-sticker philosophy that says, "I don't get mad, I get even!"? Do we Christians have available to us some sort of *spiritual anesthetic* that dulls our pain? Are we called to live as Stoics?

The Apostle Peter wrote to Christians who were living lives of pain and suffering. What kind of hope—what kind of direction—did the Holy Spirit lead him to give to these precious sufferers? Peter wrote,

> *For it is commendable if a man bears up under the pain of unjust suffering because he is conscious of God. But how is it to your credit if you receive a beating for doing wrong and endure it? But if you suffer for doing good and you endure it, this is commendable before God. To this you were called,* because Christ suffered for you, leaving you an example, that you should follow in His steps. *"He committed no sin, and no deceit was found in His mouth." When they hurled insults at Him, He did not retaliate; when He suffered, He made no threats. Instead,* He entrusted Himself to Him who judges justly (1 Peter 2:19-23, emphasis added).

Jesus suffered. In fact, His life was *characterized* by suffering. How did Jesus respond to this pain? Isaiah had prophesied of Messiah's suffering, and Peter had Isaiah 53:9 in mind, no doubt, when he wrote that Jesus "committed no sin." Jesus never did anything wrong. He never sinned. This is a clear teaching of the New Testament writers about our Lord.[1] Jesus suffered in multiple ways, yet He never responded to those who hurt Him by re-sorting to sinful retaliation. Pilate could find no sin in Jesus. One of the thieves on the cross declared Jesus to be innocent of all wrong. Peter, who spent much time with Jesus and saw Him in a variety of situations, could also vouch that Jesus never sinned. Jesus never "fought fire with fire." He never responded to suffering—even undeserved suffering—with sinful retaliation.

Continuing his quotation from Isaiah 53:9, Peter also noted, "No deceit was found in His mouth." We all can passionately agree with this observation from James, "We all stumble in many ways. If anyone is never at fault in what he says, he is a perfect man" (James 3:2). Surely, Jesus was a "perfect man." Even when He was suffering severely, Jesus never sought to protect Himself or alleviate His pain by resorting to lies or deceit.

Peter then adds this personal observation, "When they hurled their insults at Him, He did not retaliate" (1 Peter 2:23). Think of some of the horrendous insults that were hurled at the sin-less One during His earthly mission. He was called, among other things, Samaritan, glutton, drunkard, blasphemer, demon-pos-sessed, deceiver of the people, and a friend of sinners. We wonder whether Peter overheard the insults coming from the religious leaders as he stood in the high priest's courtyard on that dreadful night of betrayal. Concerning that night of abuse, Mark records, "The chief priests *accused him [Jesus] of many things.* So again Pilate asked Him, 'Aren't you going to answer? See how many things they are accusing you of.' But *Jesus still made no reply,* and Pilate was amazed" (Mark 15:3-5, emphasis added).

As our Savior hung on the cross, these same vicious people continued their assault, this time joined by the crowds who came to gawk and verbally spew their hatred upon Jesus.

> *Those who passed by* hurled insults at Him, *shaking their heads and saying, "So! You who are going to destroy the temple and build it in three days, come down from the cross and save yourself." In the same way the chief priests and the teachers of*

the law mocked him *among themselves. "He saved others," they said, "but he can't save himself! Let this Christ, this king of Israel, come down now from the cross, that we may see and believe." Those crucified with Him also* heaped insults *on Him* (Mark 15:29-32, emphasis added).

Yet our Lord never retaliated.

Imagine how you would feel if people were adding to your already excruciating pain by hurling their insults at you—insults and mockery that you knew were untrue and undeserved. Each of us must ask, *"How would I have responded?"*

Peter adds, "When He suffered, *He made no threats"* (1 Peter 2:23, emphasis added). As Matthew describes, on that horrible morning, Jesus was flogged, stripped, mocked, spit upon, and beaten on His thorn-crowned head (Matthew 27:26-31). None of this suffering was deserved. He had done nothing to hurt those people who were hurting Him. Yet, though He was severely hurting—and that, unjustly—"He made no threats." Instead of retaliating threats, the words flowing from the lips of our suffering Savior, were *"Father, forgive them"* (Luke 23:34, emphasis added).

How could He *do* that? How could Jesus take all that horrible suffering without retaliating? He certainly felt the pain. He was not anesthetized physically, emotionally, or spiritually. How could He bear up "under the pain of unjust suffering?" The key to understanding this aspect of our Lord's life is found in this one short phrase, *"Instead, He entrusted himself to Him who judges justly"* (1 Peter 2:23, emphasis added).

How Jesus *Did* Respond to Suffering

Jesus responded in *faith*. We usually think of putting our faith *in* Jesus. We don't usually think of Jesus Himself as *having* faith. Yet here is an explicit expression of Jesus responding to His many experiences of pain by "entrusting Himself" to His heavenly Father. This was no grim resignation on Jesus' part, but it was a willful choice He made. He chose to take His painful situations and entrust them—entrust *Himself*—to His trustworthy Father.

Rather than seeking to alleviate the pain He was feeling, He took His pain to the One who truly cared. Rather than seeking to take justice into His own hands, He put His faith in the One who "judges justly." Even though Jesus had the power and the right to retaliate, He chose not to. Jesus had faith in His Father and was sure that His Father would do the right thing at the right time. As the Apostle Paul wrote, "Do not repay anyone evil for evil… Do not take revenge, my friends, but leave room for God's wrath, for it is written, 'It is mine to avenge; I will repay' says the Lord" (Romans 12:17 and 19).

How Do We Respond to Suffering?

What about you and me? As citizens of this era between the lost Paradise of Eden and the yet-to-be-revealed Paradise of the New Heavens and the New Earth, we also are "familiar with suffering." Suffering is a sad reality on this fallen, sin-filled planet. Let's be frank. Some of the pain we experience is deserved. We ask for a good bit of the trouble we encounter. Unlike our Savior, we are not yet sinless. Many of our sufferings are the result of our own sinful choices and pursuits. But on the other hand, there are times when we undergo suffering that we haven't "asked for." Sometimes we experience physical, emotional, or relational suffering through no fault of our own. We live in a sinful world, encountering sinful people as we go about daily life in our communities, our workplaces, our schools, and even in our own homes.

How should we respond to suffering? How can we bear up under the pain of unjust suffering? Has Christ called us to be Christian Stoics? To be people who feel no pain? Are we supposed to "praise the Lord, anyway," by just acting as though the pain doesn't affect us *real* Christians? Or, maybe we Christians should complain, "Hey, we don't deserve to be treated like this!" drawing inward, sulking, and moping through life.

Should Christians protest by proclaiming, *"We won't be door-mats anymore!"*? Do we have a right to "get even"? Should we retaliate? Threaten? Slander those who have slandered us? Those can be very appealing options when we are suffering unjustly.

The answer comes ringing in our ears from the words of Peter, "To this you were called, because *Christ suffered for you, leaving you an example that you should follow in His steps*" (1 Peter 2:21, emphasis added). The apostle was led by the Holy Spirit to use a word for "example" that means *"copyhead."* In that era, when a child was learning to write, the teacher would place at the top of the child's exercise slate or tablet the letters or words he was to learn. The child was required to carefully copy—to "trace"—the examples placed there by his teacher. Using this kind of imagery, Peter says that God wants us to "trace" the example of our suffering Savior.

Contrary to much of the popular Christianity presented here in the West, Christians are *not* called to live free from pain. In fact, just the opposite is true. We are called by our Lord to "trace" the lifestyle of our suffering leader. We are to "follow in His steps," even as those steps lead us into a life *"familiar with suffering."*

How Will We be Able to Respond to Suffering Like Jesus Did?

How will we ever be able to endure lives characterized by unjust suffering? How are we to respond to the thoughtless employer who makes going to work drudgery instead of joy? How are we to take the humiliation that comes from the teacher or coach who seems to have it in for us? Or what if our own family members make life painfully difficult through the sinful way they treat us? The answer to these crucially important and painfully real questions is found in realizing that we are called not only to suffer, but to *respond* to our suffering in the same way Jesus did.

Following in the steps of our Savior means that we, too, must "entrust ourselves to Him who judges justly" when we experience the suffering that comes from living in this sinful world. We are to be like Jesus by taking our painful situations to our heavenly Father and entrusting them—entrusting ourselves—to Him. Instead of taking matters into our own hands and seeking retaliation against those who hurt us, we are called to follow Jesus by responding in *faith*—faith in our heavenly Father who loves us and who will do what is right with our situations in His own way and in His own time.

Can we entrust ourselves to our Heavenly Father? As Jerry Bridges wisely reminds us, "The whole idea of trusting God is, of course, based on the fact that God is absolutely trustworthy."[2] Jesus believed that. He knew that His Heavenly Father was trustworthy, so He readily entrusted Himself and His suffering "to him who judges justly" (1 Peter 2:23).

Are we ready to follow in the footsteps of our suffering Savior, entrusting ourselves and our suffering, even as He did, to our trustworthy Heavenly Father?

Our Father is omniscient. He knows all about our pain.

Our Father is omnipotent. He is able to deal with our suffering.

Our Father is all wise. He knows the best way to handle our difficulties.

Our Father is all loving. He cares about us in our trials.

Let us entrust ourselves to Him.

> *Dear friends, do not be surprised at the painful trial*
> *you are suffering,*
> *as though something strange were happening to you.*
> *But rejoice that you participate in the sufferings of Christ,*
> *so that you may be overjoyed when his glory is revealed.*
> *If you are insulted because of the name of Christ,*
> *you are blessed, for the Spirit of glory and of God rests on you.*
> *So then, those who suffer according to God's will*
> *should commit themselves to their faithful Creator*
> *and continue to do good.*
> *– 1 Peter 4:12-14 & 19*

Notes:

[1] See John 8:46; 2 Corinthians 5:21; Hebrews 4:15; 1 Peter 1:19 and 1 John 3:5.

[2] Jerry Bridges, *Trusting God* (Colorado Springs: Navpress, 1988), p. 197.

DISCUSSION QUESTIONS
SUFFERING LIKE JESUS DID

1. What aspects of Jesus' living a life "familiar with suffering" struck you afresh as you read this chapter?

2. What might be some ways we suffer because of our own sinful choices?

3. What might be some examples of ways we suffer through no fault of our own?

4. What are some common responses when we suffer through no fault of our own?

5. Why do we sometimes struggle with "entrusting ourselves to him who judges justly" when going through difficult times?

6. What are some ways in which we can grow in trusting God with our pain?

7. Think of some aspect of suffering that is on your heart. Talk to God openly about it. Ask Him to help you "entrust it" to Him. "Cast all your anxiety on him because he cares for you" (1 Peter 5:7).

Chapter Nine

PERSEVERING LIKE JESUS DID

A Model of Perseverance

He sat there shivering. The subterranean dungeon of Rome's Mamartine prison was cold and damp. He was lonely. Except for his old friend, Luke, everyone else had abandoned him. And, even though he had not really done anything wrong, he was chained like a criminal.

Many of his old friends would have viewed this situation as *tragic*. What a wasted life! The young rabbi had such a promising future ahead of him. But, somehow, he had become consumed with this Jesus of Nazareth. He had thrown away a promising future as a Jewish rabbi and had become a traveling preacher for this new religion. Where did it get him? He was now an old man, sitting in this subterranean dungeon in Rome, awaiting his execution. What a shame! What a wasted life!

This old, shivering man, chained in this cave-like, dimly-lit dungeon is writing something. He's writing his last letter to his dear "son-in-the-faith," Timothy. What is he writing? Is he writing a complaint about his poor conditions? Is he writing words of despair and regret? Let's look over Paul's shoulder as he writes his departing words to his spiritual son: "For I am already being poured out like a drink offering, and the time has come for my departure. I have fought the good fight, *I have finished the race*, I have kept the faith. Now there is in store for me the crown of righteousness, which the Lord, the righteous Judge, will award to me on that day…" (2 Timothy 4:6-8, emphasis added).

These are not words of regret, but of grateful victory. Paul was about to cross the finish line of his marathon of serving Christ. The run had been difficult. He had endured beatings, imprisonment, shipwreck, and abandonment.[1] But, he had endured. He had *persevered*.

Our Perseverance

The apostle Paul is not the only Christian called to persevere in the marathon of the Christian life. All of us are included in the exhortation of Hebrews 12:1-3:

> *Therefore, since we are surrounded by such a great cloud of witnesses, let us throw off everything that hinders and the sin that so easily entangles, and let us run with perseverance the race marked out for us. Let us fix our eyes on Jesus, the author and perfecter of our faith, who for the joy set before him endured the cross, scorning its shame, and sat down at the right hand of the throne of God. Consider him who endured such opposition from sinful men, so that you will not grow weary and lose heart.*

The Christian life is pictured as a race that is to be run with *perseverance*. This race is a marathon, not a sprint, and the course is already laid out for us. We do not have the liberty to run along whatever course we feel like taking. The race of the Christian life has been "marked out for us" by God. We had better make sure we are on the right track! Jesus said, "Enter through the narrow gate. For wide is the gate and broad is the road that leads to destruction, and *many* enter through it. But small is the gate and *narrow the road that leads to life, and only a few find it*" (Matthew 7:13-14, emphasis added).

There is only one track that leads to eternal life. Jesus explained, "*I am the way* and the truth and the life. *No one comes to the Father except through me*" (John 14:6, emphasis added). So, as we consider our marathon, we must first make sure we are on the right course—the course that leads to eternal life. That will mean making sure all our hope and trust for eternal life are securely fixed on Him, the "author and perfecter of our faith" (Hebrews 12:2).

We are counseled to run our race "*with perseverance.*" Apparently some of the early Jewish Christians (who were the first recipients of the letter to the Hebrews) had begun their Christian race well, but were now starting to falter. Some wanted to give up following "the race marked out for us" by Jesus the Messiah, and wanted to go back to the old track of Judaism. The author of Hebrews warns them, "Don't do it! Don't get off Jesus' track. Run with endurance. *Run with perseverance!*" There must be firm resolve not to drop out of the race–a determination to cross the finish line despite hardship, opposition, exhaustion and pain. "He who stands firm [or 'perseveres']² to the end will be saved" (Matthew 10:22).

This certainly sounds like a challenging marathon, doesn't it? What counsel does the Word of God give us for running it successfully? He directs us, "Throw off everything that hinders."

Imagine standing near the starting line of an Olympic marathon. As we survey the runners gathered at the starting line, we notice one runner who has a huge backpack, and he's pulling a little red wagon piled high with *stuff.* He's got his stereo, his TV, his cell phone, his computer, his golf clubs–and who knows what else. In our astonishment, we call out to him, "What are you doing with all that *stuff?*" He answers, "Well, I just don't know what I'd do without all my things. I'm taking them along on my marathon today, just in case I might need them." We would rightly question the sanity of this so-called marathoner. How is he ever going to persevere in running this marathon if he is dragging along all these unnecessary things?

Yet, look at our own attempts to run the marathon of the Christian life. Are we dragging along unnecessary *stuff* that will accomplish little more than bogging us down? These may be things that are not necessarily sinful, in and of themselves, but neither are they helping us in running our race. They are "excess baggage."

Do we need to shed some excess baggage in the form of *bad habits*? For example, excessive TV watching can suck up huge portions of time. Are such habits helping us run our race, or slowing us down? Are there other bad habits hindering our running that we need to "throw off"?

Are we running with some *wrong priorities*? Do we look back over the previous week and ask ourselves, "Where did all my time go?" Have we been spending time on activities that do little to help us in running our race? Maybe we should include in our morning prayer times, "Lord, what do you want me *not* to do today?" Such prayers may help us throw off those things that hinder us in running the Christian marathon.

Have we acquired possessions or added activities to our already-busy lives that make running Christian life more difficult? So often we approach possessions or activities by asking ourselves, "Is this *allowable* for a Christian?" Maybe we should ask ourselves instead, "Will this activity or possession *hinder* me or *help* me in running the race?" We may be able to run our races better without those added activities or possessions.

The author of Hebrews continues his counsel in chapter 12, verse 1 with, "throw off...the sin that so easily entangles." In the context of the book of Hebrews, the primary entangling sin is that of "unbelief." A *lack of faith*—a distrust in God's Word—can easily trip us up when we encounter difficulties along the marathon of life. We can begin to doubt that following Christ is really worth the effort. We begin to question whether He really cares about our situation. This lack of faith saps the spiritual energy right out of us.

Obviously, many other sins can trip us up as well. The lust for pleasure, power, and possessions can all "entangle us" as we try to run our race. Let us "throw off" all these sins that are entangling us. John Bunyan, the author of the classic *Pilgrim's Progress*, advised Christians how to respond when the sins of the world call to us, seeking to distract us and get us off course: "Let me alone…come not nigh [near] me, for I am running for heaven…If I win, I win all, and if I lose, I lose all; let me alone, for I will not hear!"[3]

What *encouragements* does God provide in His Word to help us run the marathon of the Christian life successfully and with perseverance?

The Perseverance of the Old Testament Saints

Hebrews 12:1 encourages us with, "*Therefore*, since we are surrounded by such a great cloud of witnesses" (emphasis added). The "therefore" points us back to chapter eleven—the great "Hall of Faith," that depicts the perseverance of so many Old Testament saints. People such as Noah, Abraham and Sarah, Joseph, Moses, and Rahab testify that the life of faith can indeed be run successfully. All these Old Testament people who persisted through great difficulties now serve as encouraging examples of perseverance. They are no mere spectators to our race, but are "witnesses" of what can be done through faith in God. These are the runners who have successfully completed the race and now testify to us that, by God's grace, we too, can persevere in running our race. It's as if the crowd of Old Testament saints calls to us from the far side of the finish line, "Run the race! Don't give up! Run with perseverance! It will be worth it all on that great day when you cross the finish line!"

Jesus: The Ultimate Example of Perseverance

But one model and motivator to perseverance stands out in the crowd of those who have already completed the race. The author of Hebrews encourages us, "Let us fix our eyes on *Jesus*" (Hebrews 12:2, emphasis added). Like the athlete who fixes his eyes on the goal and never looks back—never becomes distracted by things off to the side—so we are to run our race with our eyes fixed on Jesus.

Jesus is the "author and perfecter" of our faith. Jesus ran the race, too. He blazed the trail and reached the goal. In that sense, He is the "author" of our race. And, Jesus is also the "perfecter"of our faith. He lived His entire earthly life in faithfulness to His heavenly Father. He never got off track. He never quit. He successfully ran the race the Father marked out for Him, and thus secured our faith. He is our "Champion."

Deuteronomy 21:23 teaches us, "Anyone who is hung on a tree is under God's curse." The cross was a shameful thing. In hanging on the cross, Jesus had all the sins of His people placed on His innocent body. He had to endure the unspeakable pain of having His heavenly Father turn His face away, but this was the "race set before *Him*." Isaiah had prophesied hundreds of years before that He would be "stricken by God, smitten by Him and afflicted...pierced...crushed...[and wounded]" (Isaiah 53:4-5). Still, Jesus *persevered*. Jesus "endured the cross, scorning the shame" (Hebrews 12:2). Though His race was immeasurably more difficult than our race, Jesus persevered.

Humanly speaking, Jesus could have quit. He could have quit His race in the wilderness, buckling to the temptations of Satan.[4] He could have quit in Nazareth the day His neighbors rejected Him and sought to kill Him.[5] He could have quit in the Garden of Gethsemane as He was overwhelmed in the anguish of His soul.[6] However, Jesus didn't quit. He persevered to the end of His race.

The night before Jesus died on the cross, He reported to His Father, "I have brought you glory on earth by *completing* the work you gave me to do" (John 17:4, emphasis added). As He gave His dying breath that next day, He cried out in victory, "*It is finished!*" (John 19:30, emphasis added). And, having finished His race, "He sat down at the right hand of the throne of God" (Hebrews 12:2), a picture of triumphant perseverance.

Our Commitment to Persevere

Our race may be difficult, but we are called to run with *perseverance*. Many other believers over the centuries have successfully stayed the course and completed their races. We are "surrounded by such a great cloud of witnesses" (Hebrews 12:1), reminding us of God's faithfulness in enabling us to finish the race.

But above all other encouragements to endure is the confidence we gain by fixing our eyes on Jesus, "the author and perfecter of our faith." He completed His race, thus enabling us to complete ours. "Consider him, who endured such opposition from sinful men, so that you do not grow weary and lose heart" (Hebrews 12:3). Let us continue to "run with perseverance the race marked out for us" with our eyes firmly fixed on Jesus.

Through many dangers, toils and snares,
I have already come;
'Tis grace has brought me safe thus far,
And grace will lead me home.
And when this flesh and heart shall fail;
And mortal life shall cease,
I shall possess within the veil
A life of joy and peace.
- From John Newton's "Amazing Grace"

Notes:

[1] See 2 Corinthians 11:23-29 for a more full recounting of the sufferings Paul endured during his life of ministry.

[2] The Greek word for "stands firm" in Matthew 10:22 has the same root as the word translated "perseverance" in Hebrews 12:1.

[3] John Bunyan, *The Whole Works of John Bunyan, Volume III* (Grand Rapids, MI: Baker Book House, 1977 reprint), p. 386.

[4] See Luke 4:1-13.

[5] For this full story, see Luke 4:14-30.

[6] See Matthew 26:36-46.

DISCUSSION QUESTIONS
PERSEVERING LIKE JESUS DID

1. What are some practical ideas for keeping the *goal
   of successfully finishing our race* in view as we run the
   marathon of the Christian life day-by-day?

2. Consider the "stuff" of your life. What excess baggage
   (in the form of bad habits, wrong priorities, or lack of
   faith) is slowing you down as you "run the race"? What do
   you believe God is calling you to do with the "stuff" that is
   hindering you in your Christian life?

3. What might be some indicators that a Christian
   friend is beginning to waver in his or her commitment to
   persevere in following Christ? Read Hebrews 3:12-14 as you
   prayerfully consider your ministry to this wavering friend.

4. Who is one of your favorite Bible characters who
   "persevered" in his or her commitment to the Lord? What is
   there about his or her life that encourages you to persevere
   in your own Christian race?

5. How can our churches be more faithful in encouraging
   a long-range view to the Christian life—that it's not a
   "sprint" but a "marathon" that must be run to the end?

6. This week, spend some time with God, asking Him
   to point out to you any specific hindrances or sinful
   entanglements that are slowing you down in your spiritual
   progress. Ask the Lord to help you "throw them off," so you
   will not "grow weary and lose heart."

Chapter Ten

PRACTICING PATIENCE
LIKE JESUS DID

They killed Stephen that day. Filled with the Holy Spirit, Stephen had preached powerfully of Jesus Christ as Lord and Savior. The religious establishment was furious. So, they dragged Stephen just outside the city walls of Jerusalem and threw rocks at him until his body lay dead beside the road—bloodied and broken. *"And Saul was there, giving approval to his death"* (Acts 8:1, emphasis added).

That's how we meet this promising young rabbi known as Saul of Tarsus: standing near the dead body of Stephen, apparently with a smug smile on his face now that this preaching deacon would no longer be speaking of Jesus Christ. Acts 8 adds more dark colors to the portrait of Saul: "Godly men buried Stephen and mourned deeply for him. But *Saul began to destroy the church.* Going from house to house, he dragged off men and women and put them in prison" (Acts 8:2-3, emphasis added).

And the portrait gets darker. "*Saul was still breathing out murderous threats* against the Lord's disciples. He went to the high priest and asked him for letters to the synagogues in Damascus, so that if he found any there who belonged to the Way, whether men or women, he might take them as prisoners to Jerusalem" (Acts 9:1-2, emphasis added).

The picture of Saul of Tarsus as an enemy of Jesus Christ and of His people is not one conjured up by those who had some vendetta against him. By his own mouth he would later confess,

I too was convinced that I ought to do all that was possible to oppose the name of Jesus of Nazareth. And that is just what I did in Jerusalem. On the authority of the chief priests I put many of the saints in prison, and when they were put to death, I cast my vote against them. Many a time I went from one synagogue to another to have them punished, and I tried to force them to blaspheme. In my obsession against them, I even went to foreign cities to persecute them (Acts 26:9-11).

Would you want this man living in your neighborhood? Saul had an obsessive hatred of Jesus Christ and everyone who professed to be His follower. It didn't matter whether you were a man or a woman, he would travel great distances to arrest you and throw you into prison. He would do whatever he could to force people to recant their faith in Jesus Christ. And, if the court was deciding whether you should live or die, he would vote for the death sentence every time.

Here's a question worth pondering: *Why didn't Jesus stop him?* Why did Jesus tolerate this nearly demonic persecutor of the early church? Why didn't Jesus stop him in his obsession to destroy the lives of those early church members?

According to the testimony of Saul (now known as "Paul"), Jesus *did* stop him one day. Listen in as Paul remembers the day he encountered Jesus Christ. "On one of those journeys I was going to Damascus with the authority and commission of the chief priests. About noon…as I was on the road, I saw a light from heaven, brighter than the sun, blazing around me and my companions. We all fell to the ground, and I heard a voice saying to me in Aramaic, 'Saul, Saul, why do you persecute me?'" (Acts 26:12-14).

Is Jesus finally going to crush this persecutor of the church? Is Jesus going to stomp on this proud Pharisee like a cockroach? Let's find out.

> *Then I asked, "Who are you, Lord?" "I am Jesus,*
> *whom you are persecuting," the Lord replied. "Now*
> *get up and stand on your feet. I have appeared to*
> *you to appoint you as a servant and as a witness of*
> *what you have seen of me and what I will show you.*
> *I will rescue you from your own people and from*
> *the Gentiles. I am sending you to them to open their*
> *eyes and turn them from darkness to light, and from*
> *the power of Satan to God, so that they may receive*
> *forgiveness of sins and a place among those who are*
> *sanctified by faith in me"* (Acts 26:15-18).

Did you catch that? Instead of crushing this man obsessed with destroying the church, Jesus is going to make him a missionary! Why would Jesus do that? Thought-provoking question, isn't it? Why would Jesus tolerate this violent, calloused, self-righteous, bigoted persecutor of the church for so long, and then finally intervene—not to crush him—but to save him and make him a missionary of the gospel?

The answer to that probing question is found, not in the person of Paul, but in the person of Jesus Christ. Paul wrote this explanation to his protégé, Timothy: "Here is a trustworthy saying that deserves full acceptance: Christ Jesus came into the world to save sinners—of whom I am the worst. *But for that very reason I was shown mercy so that in me, the worst of sinners, Christ Jesus might display his unlimited patience* as an example for those who would believe on him and receive eternal life" (1 Timothy 1:15-16, emphasis added).

Twice in that paragraph to Timothy, Paul referred to himself as "the worst of sinners." No doubt many people today read that self-assessment and think, "Oh, come on Paul. You're just trying to be humble. You weren't that bad. In fact, there are lots of people who were worse sinners than you!" But shouldn't we take Paul seriously? Why try to talk Paul out of this self-assessment? In that same letter to Timothy he referred to his life-before-Christ as being that of a "blasphemer and a persecutor and a violent man" (1 Timothy 1:13). Paul (then, Saul) really had been guilty of blaspheming the name of Christ and persecuting the very people who had been purchased with the blood of Jesus—committing great violence against the precious sons and daughters of the High King of heaven.

I wonder if Paul had nightmares of his past sins against Christ and His church. I wonder if he could see the bloody, broken body of Stephen lying there along the road. I wonder if he could hear in his memory the sound of children crying as their Christian parents were being hauled off to jail. As Paul thought of his past, it's as if he were saying, "If you were to line up all the sinners of the world in order of their offenses, I would be in the front row!"

Yet, how did Jesus treat this blasphemer? This violent persecutor of the church? This "worst of sinners"? Rather than crushing this insolent troublemaker, Jesus showed him mercy and grace. To quote Paul's own testimony, "The grace of our Lord was poured out on me abundantly" (1 Timothy 1:14). That day on the road near Damascus, Saul of Tarsus was saved by the amazing, sovereign grace of Jesus Christ. Jesus showed him mercy in the very midst of his obsessive violence against Christians.

Amazingly, Jesus not only saved this destructive persecutor from the hell he deserved, but He also made him a very useful instrument in the advancement of the great missionary endeavor of that day (1 Timothy 1:12). I wonder if, after a long day of ministry, Paul might lie on his bed at night with tears of astonished gratitude wetting his pillow as he prayed,

> *Dear Jesus, thank you so much for taking this mouth that used to blaspheme your holy name and breathe out murderous threats and filling it with sweet messages of your grace. Dear Jesus, thank you for taking this hard and hateful heart that was so full of animosity toward you and your precious children and filling it with a passion to know you and to love your dear people. Thank you, dear Jesus, for taking this proud Pharisee so bent on*

destroying your church and using me to build up
your kingdom all over the world. Your grace is so
amazing, precious Jesus. I love you. Amen.

So, why did Jesus do it? Why did He show mercy and grace to this "worst of sinners"? He had a reason, and that reason focused not so much on Saul, the receiver of grace, as it did on Jesus, the giver of grace. What was Jesus' reason for choosing to show mercy and grace to Saul of Tarsus? Notice what Paul [Saul] wrote in his personal testimony of salvation: "But for that very reason I was shown mercy so that in me, the worst of sinners, Christ Jesus might display his unlimited patience…" (1 Timothy 1:16).

Jesus chose to save this "worst of sinners" in order to put on display one of His amazing attributes—His "patience." Instead of crushing this murderous persecutor, Jesus tolerated him day after painful day, week after painful week, month after painful month. And then, one day, wonder of wonders, Jesus poured out His mercy and grace on Saul of Tarsus.

What does Jesus' patience have to do with you and me?

The Patience of Jesus Means Our Salvation

Paul was not an exceptional case. In fact, the Bible says that Paul was an example—a prototype—of the kind of people Jesus chooses to save in order to put His amazing patience on display. 1 Timothy 1:16 explains that Jesus chose to save Saul of Tarsus [Paul], "as *an example* [of] those who would believe on him and receive eternal life" (emphasis added). This is such an important truth that it became a "trustworthy saying" in the early church. "Here is a trustworthy saying that deserves full acceptance: *Christ Jesus came into the world to save sinners*" (1 Timothy 1:15, emphasis added).

Every Christian should look back at his life before Christ saved him and ask, "Why didn't the Lord crush me as I was rebelling against Him? Why did He not send me to hell long ago?" Peter explained it this way, "He is *patient* with you, not wanting anyone to perish, but everyone to come to repentance" (2 Peter 3:9, emphasis added) and "Bear in mind that *our Lord's patience means salvation*" (2 Peter 3:15, emphasis added). If you are a true follower of Jesus Christ, your life serves as a canvas on which Jesus has painted a portrait of His own character—specifically His attribute of *patience*.

The Patience of Jesus Is the Model of How We Should Treat Other People

Jesus' patience is put on display not only in our initial salvation, but also in how He continues to bear with us in our daily sins. Charles Spurgeon reminds us,

> *It is a great act of eternal love when Christ once for all absolves the sinner and puts him into the family of God; but* what condescending patience there is when the Saviour with much long-suffering bears the oft recurring follies of his wayward disciple; *day by day, and hour by hour, washing away the multiplied transgressions of his erring but beloved child! To dry up a flood of rebellion is something marvelous,* but to endure the constant dropping of repeated offences–to bear with a perpetual trying of patience, this is love indeed (emphasis added)![1]

Do our daily lives mirror the gracious patience Jesus has shown us and continues to show us? Do we reflect the patience of our Savior as we endure the daily irritations of living in a fallen world? Do we respond patiently to the inconsiderate driver who cuts us off? The person seated next to us in the restaurant loudly conversing on her cell phone? The rude cashier at the checkout line?

Do we treat our family members with the patience Christ has shown us less-than-ideal children of God? How patient are we with noisy children? The sulking teen? The forgetful elderly relative? The spouse who sees the issue differently?

How can we better reflect the patience of our Lord at our workplaces or in our schools?

Remembering the patience Christ continues to show us, cannot we be more patient with that calloused boss who piles on the work? The teacher who shows little sympathy to the struggling student? The co-worker who isn't pulling his share of the load?

How patient are we with our fellow church members? Are we showing the patience of Christ to that person who talks too much in our Sunday School class or small group? How much of Christ's patience are we reflecting to that church member whose preferred worship style is so different from our own?

How patient are we even with our Lord who is so patient with us? Do our prayer lives demonstrate a confident patience as we take our concerns to the Lord, day after day, month after month, year after year without, apparently, seeing the answers to our requests?

Oh, how patient Jesus was with the "worst of sinners." How patient He has been with you and me! May we be grateful reflectors of His patience. "As a prisoner for Lord, then, I urge you to *live a life worthy of the calling you have received.* Be completely humble and gentle; *be patient,* bearing with one another in love" (Ephesians 4:1-2, emphasis added).

Dear Lord, how You could be so patient with me, I cannot comprehend. I have ignored You, disobeyed You, and placed You on the periphery of my life. Thank you for not treating me as my sins deserve, but showing me Your saving patience. Help me, Lord, to reflect to the people I encounter in everyday life the patience You have shown me.

> *Therefore, as God's chosen people,*
> *holy and dearly loved,*
> *clothe yourselves with compassion,*
> *kindness, humility, gentleness,*
> *and patience.*
> – Colossians 3:12

Note:

[1] Charles Spurgeon, *Morning and Evening*, (Ross-shire, Scotland: Christian Focus Publications Ltd., 1997 reprint), October 24, evening.

DISCUSSION QUESTIONS
PRACTICING PATIENCE LIKE JESUS DID

1. How did Jesus show His patience with you before you were saved?

2. Why did Jesus save you? Which of His attributes does He put on display when He saves ill-deserving sinners like you and me?

3. In what situations do you most often show impatience?

4. How does Christ's patience toward you impact how you treat other people whom you find "trying"?

5. Think right now of someone with whom you find it especially difficult to be patient. Pray for God's blessing upon that person. Ask God to give you opportunities to show Christlike patience to him or her.

Chapter Eleven

FORGIVING LIKE JESUS DID

"Father, *forgive them*, for they do not know what they are doing" (Luke 23:34, emphasis added). What was going through the minds of the Roman soldiers standing guard at that horrible place of Jesus' crucifixion just outside the walls of Jerusalem? The veteran soldiers had no doubt heard a variety of words from the mouths of those being crucified. Sometimes they had heard the loud curses of enraged criminals as they were subjected to that terrifying means of execution. At other times the soldiers had heard pitiful cries for mercy from the lips of those being crucified. But never had they heard anything like this.

"Father, *forgive them*, for they do not know what they are do-ing." What were the religious leaders of the Jews thinking? Some of them had come out to the place of execution to make sure that this troublemaker, Jesus of Nazareth, really did get His due. Did the assured smirks on their faces suddenly turn to confused frowns as they pondered the meaning of such an unexpected prayer from the very one whose execution they had manipulated? *"Father, for-give them"*? How could He pray such a prayer at such a time?

What Is Forgiveness?

Our English dictionaries tell us that "to forgive" means "to give up resentment against an offender, to give up a desire to punish, or to stop being angry with someone."[1] The Greek word used in Luke 23:34 is the most common word for "forgiveness."[2]

The root concept seems to be "letting go" or "giving it up." We can think of "forgiveness" as "letting go of the desire for vengeance or retaliation." Forgiveness is a choice or a decision to "let go" of the desire to hold grudges or to get even when someone hurts us.

Whom Did Jesus Forgive?

Jesus forgave people who were truly sorry—people who were repentant for their sins. We remember the story of the woman who was heartbroken over her sinful life. "When a woman who had lived a sinful life in that town learned that Jesus was eating at the Pharisee's house, she brought an alabaster jar of perfume, and as she stood behind him at His feet weeping, she began to wet His feet with her tears. Then she wiped them with her hair, kissed them and poured perfume on them" (Luke 7:37-38).

Although this woman was heartbroken over her sin, the religious leaders of Jesus' day continued to look on her with disdain. But how did Jesus see her? "Jesus said to her, 'Your sins are forgiven'" (Luke 7:48). Jesus freely forgave *repentant sinners*.

Jesus also forgave His enemies. He forgave even people who were *not* sorry for their sins—people who had not even asked for forgiveness. As Jesus was being nailed to the cross, His first public utterance was those astonishing words, "Father, forgive them." For whom was Jesus asking forgiveness? Jesus was asking the Father to forgive the Jewish leaders—the very people who had twisted His teaching, slandered His character and insisted upon His crucifixion. Jesus was asking the Father also to forgive the Roman soldiers who had so horribly abused Him with rods, whips, fists, and the crown of thorns. It was the Roman soldiers who had beaten Jesus' body into a bloody pulp. It was the Roman soldiers who had just pounded those spikes through His hands and feet. And now it was those Roman soldiers for whom Jesus was asking forgiveness.

Jesus was asking the Father to forgive the crowd, gathered and gawking at the foot of the cross. As the jeering spectators were spewing out words of hatred and mockery, Jesus was at that very time asking His heavenly Father to forgive them.

We might expect Jesus' prayer to be something like, "Father, make them stop hurting Me! Father, I don't deserve this abuse! Pour out Your wrath right now on these people who are abusing Me and mocking Me! Send Your judgment on these crucifiers!" But instead, we clearly hear the Savior pray, "Father, *forgive* them."

Isn't that amazing? Sometimes we have difficulty forgiving people who ask us for forgiveness. Sometimes we withhold forgiveness even from people who are truly sorry for how they have hurt us. But we see Jesus forgiving His abusers while they were in the process of murdering Him! They were not broken over their sin. They were not asking for forgiveness. Yet, Jesus prayed for His Father to forgive them. The prophecy of Isaiah 53:12 takes on flesh: "For He bore the sins of many and made intercession for the transgressors."

Why Was Jesus so Forgiving?

The answer to this critical question is not found in the people He forgave. They certainly did not deserve His forgiveness. The answer to the mind-boggling question, "Why was Jesus so forgiving?" is found in Jesus Himself.

Jesus was forgiving *because His mission of coming to the earth was to reveal to us the character of the Father.* The Father is a forgiving God.

> *The LORD is compassionate and gracious,*
> *slow to anger, abounding in love.*
> *He will not always accuse,*
> *nor will he harbor his anger forever;*
> *he does not treat us as our sins deserve*
> *or repay us according to our iniquities.*
> *For as high as the heavens are above the earth,*
> *so great is his love for those who fear him;*
> *as far as the east is from the west,*
> *so far has he removed our transgressions from us.*
> *– Psalm 103:8-12*

Jesus was the embodiment here on earth of this forgiving God.

Jesus also was forgiving in order to fulfill another of His purposes in coming to this sinful earth. The Apostle Paul said it succinctly, "Here is a trustworthy saying that deserves full acceptance: Christ Jesus came into the world to save sinners" (1 Timothy 1:15). All of us who are the undeserving recipients of that forgiveness are eternally grateful.

What about Us?

As Christians, our guide for daily living is, "This is how we know we are in Him: Whoever claims to live in him must walk as Jesus did" (1 John 2:5b-6). How does this impact us in the realm of being "forgiving people" as we live daily life in our homes, schools, jobs, churches and communities? Colossians 3:13 is clear, "Forgive as the Lord forgave you." The basis of our being a forgiving people is not how we are treated by other people, but how Christ has already treated us. He forgave us of our innumerable offenses. Standing on the sure footing of His forgiveness, we can then forgive those who hurt us. "Bear with each other and forgive whatever grievances you may have against one another. *Forgive as the Lord forgave you*" (Colossians 3:13, emphasis added). There is no room for bitterness in the heart of a follower of the forgiving Jesus Christ. There is no place for grudges—no justification for getting even in the daily life of a person who has experienced the astonishing forgiveness of the Lord Jesus.

As people who have personally experienced the forgiveness of Christ, we must forgive not only those people who humbly come to us asking our forgiveness, but like our Lord, we also must forgive those who hurt us and never come seeking forgiveness. Jesus clearly directed us, "Love your enemies and pray for those who persecute you" (Matthew 5:44).

Why Should We Forgive Those Who Hurt Us?

You might be struggling as you read this. "Oh, but you don't know how that person hurt me! You don't know the deep pain and scars I carry with me because of how much they hurt me.

They don't *deserve* to be forgiven! Why should I forgive someone who has hurt me so?"

Why should we forgive? The answer to that heart-searching question is not found in the worthiness of the offender. Often we hold back forgiveness, justifying our stubbornness with "Well, she doesn't deserve to be forgiven because of how badly she hurt me. There's no way I could forgive her after what she did to me!"

This kind of response approaches the problem from the wrong direction. We must forgive because we have been forgiven. "Be kind and compassionate to one another, *just as in Christ God forgave you*" (Ephesians 4:32, emphsis added).

Another reason we should forgive others is that we want *to be forgiven*. Jesus was explicit: "For if you forgive men when they sin against you, your heavenly Father will also forgive you. But if you do not forgive men their sins, your Father will not forgive your sins" (Matthew 6:14-15). Every professing Christian must ask himself, "Would I want Jesus to treat me the same way I have treated others? Would I want Him to be as forgiving to me as I have been to those who have sinned against me?"

Making this painful point to His Galilean listeners, Jesus told a story that has become known as "The Parable of the Unmerciful Servant" (see Matthew 18:21-35). In this story, a servant of a king was unable to pay a large debt he owed his master. The king took pity on the man and forgave his unpayable debt. Sadly, this same servant refused to forgive a much smaller debt owed him by a fellow servant. When the king heard about his hardheartedness, he called him in a second time and rebuked him. "'You wicked servant,' he said, 'I canceled all that debt of yours because you begged me to. Shouldn't you have had mercy on your fellow servant just as I had on you?'" Jesus relates, "In anger his master turned him over to the jailers to be tortured, until he should pay back all he owed." Then the Lord adds these sobering words of application, "This is how my heavenly Father will treat each of you unless you forgive your brother from your heart" (Matthew 18:32-35).

How Can We Become More Forgiving People?

First, *we must remember who our Heavenly Father is.* He knows all about our situations, and He will deal with them in His time and in His way. Often, when we take vengeance into our own hands, we are, in essence, protesting to God, "I don't like the way You are handling this. This person has hurt me, and You're not doing anything about it. *I'm taking matters into my own hands, God!*"

Can we trust God to take care of these offenses that other people commit against us? Do we trust God to take care of our painful situations? Consider what the apostle Paul wrote in Romans 12:17-19 about trusting God when we have been wronged by others. "Do not repay anyone evil for evil. Be careful to do what is right in the eyes of everybody. If it is possible, as far as it depends on you, live at peace with everyone. *Do not take revenge, my friends, but leave room for God's wrath*, for it is written: 'It is mine to avenge; I will repay,' says the Lord" (emphasis added).

Second, *we must remember whose we are.* Remember the amazing grace God has shown us in granting us forgiveness. He has freely forgiven us even though we have offended Him time and again. He has forgiven us so much. Can we not forgive the lesser sins other people commit against us? God has treated us with grace, mercy, and forgiveness. How can we treat others with bitterness, vengeance, and unforgiveness? To paraphrase our Lord, "He who has been forgiven much, forgives much."

And third, *we need to deliberately decide to show compassion to those who have hurt us.* The Bible clearly commands followers of Jesus not to seek vengeance on those who sin against us. Romans 12:20-21 directs us, "On the contrary: 'If your enemy is hungry, feed him; if he is thirsty, give him something to drink. In doing this, you will heap burning coals on his head.' Do not be overcome by evil, but overcome evil with good." Many Christians can testify how the Lord softened their hearts toward those who have hurt them as they have obeyed this directive from Romans 12. Showing compassion often changes the heart of the offended, making it easier to lovingly forgive the offender.

Every follower of Jesus has been, and will be, hurt by other people. How will we treat those who have offended us? Let us release all bitterness and *forgive, even as we have been forgiven.*

> *More about Jesus would I know,*
> *More of His grace to others show,*
> *More of His saving fullness see,*
> *More of His love who died for me.*
> *More, more about Jesus,*
> *More, more about Jesus;*
> *More of His saving fullness see,*
> *More of His love, who died for me!*
> – Eliza E. Hewitt

Notes:

[1] *Webster's New Twentieth Century Dictionary of the English Language, unabridged* (New York: Collins World, 1978), p. 720.

[2] This most common Greek word for "forgive" is ἀφίημι.

DISCUSSION QUESTIONS
FORGIVING LIKE JESUS DID

1. What is a good definition of "forgiveness"?

2. Why is it so difficult to forgive those who hurt us?

3. Why should we forgive those who hurt us or sin against us? See Colossians 3:13 and Ephesians 4:32.

4. How does our willingness to forgive others impact what we should expect on Judgment Day? Carefully read Matthew 6:14-15 before answering.

5. Read Romans 12:17-19. How many seats are behind the Judge's bench? Who is sitting on it? What are we saying about our view of God when we decide to seek vengeance instead of offering forgiveness to those who hurt us?

6. Think of someone who has hurt you. In what tangible ways can you demonstrate that you have forgiven him or her? Is there some act of compassion you can do for that person this week?

Chapter Twelve

PRAYING LIKE JESUS DID

It was very early in the morning. Simon Peter's house guest got up quietly and slipped into the cool, still-dark streets of the lakeside town of Capernaum. Making His way along the deserted lanes, He left the town and found a place where He could be alone. However, He was not really alone, because He was spending those early morning hours with His heavenly Father. Those precious hours conversing with His Father were abruptly interrupted by a concerned Peter. We can almost hear the exasperated question, "Where have You been? We've been looking for You everywhere!" (See Mark 1:35-37.)

Who was that Man devoting His early morning hours to prayer? It was Jesus. Have you ever noticed that Jesus prayed a lot? Have you ever wondered why?

What Was Jesus' Prayer Life Like?

Jesus Prayed Often

The Gospels record many accounts of Jesus praying. No doubt, Jesus prayed many other times that were never witnessed by the Gospel writers. James Stewart, professor of New Testament at Edinburgh University, observed, "Prayer was the habitual atmosphere of Jesus' daily life."[1] Consider some of the occasions in which Jesus prayed. He prayed at His baptism, at the beginning of His public ministry (Luke 3:21). He prayed before a day of busy and fruitful ministry (Mark 1:35-39). Jesus also prayed at the end of a full day of ministry and miracles (Luke 5:15-16).

Jesus prayed before making a major decision, such as the choosing of the twelve apostles (Luke 6:12). He prayed in His last few hours with His disciples (John17). He prayed the night before He went to the cross–during the time of His most severe trial in the Garden of Gethsemane (Luke 22:39-46). We also see and hear Jesus praying during the unfathomable anguish of the cross. Jesus died praying (Luke 23:34, 46).

Unlike many of His professed followers, Jesus prayed not only when people were watching and listening, but also when no one else would have noticed. Luke tells us, "But Jesus often withdrew to lonely places and prayed" (Luke 5:16). He often prayed when the only audience He had was His Heavenly Father.

Jesus Prayed Passionately

Prayer was no meaningless ritual for Jesus. Listen to Luke's description of Jesus' praying: "And being in anguish, He prayed more earnestly, and His sweat was like drops of blood falling to the ground" (Luke 22:44). The author of Hebrews reports, "He offered up prayers and petitions with loud cries and tears..." (Hebrews 5:7).

Jesus Prayed Urgently

He seemed compelled to pray. He sometimes would get up at 3:00 or 4:00 in the morning to pray (see Mark 1:35, for example). Even though Jesus led a very busy life, with many people making demands on His time, Jesus made time to pray.

Jesus Prayed at Length

At times Jesus offered up short prayers to His Heavenly Father, but on other occasions He prayed for long periods of time–sometimes for hours. In fact, Luke writes of one occasion when "Jesus went out to a mountainside to pray, and spent the night praying to God" (Luke 6:12).

Why did Jesus Pray?

Many years ago, nineteenth century author William Blaikie made an observation that no doubt expresses the feelings of many readers of the Gospel accounts. He wrote, "Beautiful though the prayerfulness of Jesus be in itself, yet when we think of who He was, it takes us somewhat by surprise."[2] Similarly, nineteenth century Baptist theologian John Broadus wrote, "If any human being was ever able to stand alone in the universe, without leaning on God, it might have been true of him [Jesus]."[3]

If there were ever a person to walk this planet who did not need to pray, it was Jesus. Yet, if there were ever a person whose life was marked by prayerfulness, it, too, was Jesus. We are confronted with this question, *"Why did Jesus pray?"*

Jesus *Wanted* to Pray

Simply put, Jesus prayed *because He wanted to.* Jesus said, "The Father loves the Son" (John 5:20). Jesus was fully assured of His Father's love, and He in turn loved His Father. Jesus sometimes prayed for "communion" or "fellowship" with His Heavenly Father who "loved [Him] before the creation of the world" (John 17:24). James Stewart noted, "Often Jesus would turn to God, not for the sake of any gift that he was needing but simply for the sake of God's own fellowship."[4]

What kind of son would talk to his father only when he wanted something? A loving son would address his father for the pure enjoyment of their personal relationship. Jesus' prayers often were addressed tenderly (and respectfully) to "Father" or "Holy Father." "Jesus loved God his Father so utterly and so passionately that he could not bear to be away from him, but used every opportunity the days and nights brought him to go and speak to the God of his love again."[5]

Jesus *Needed* to Pray

But Jesus also prayed *because He needed to.* Thoughtfully read Hebrews 5:7: "During the days of Jesus' life on earth, He offered up prayers and petitions with loud cries and tears to the one who could save Him from death, and He was heard because of His reverent submission." The phrase in the NIV "during the days of Jesus' life on earth" is literally, *"in the days of His flesh."* In other words, Jesus prayed because He was a man—a real human being.

As J. Oswald Sanders wrote, "Though truly divine, His deity in no way affected the reality of His human nature. His prayers were as real and intense as any ever offered."[6] In other words, Jesus prayed because, as a human being, He was fully aware of His dependence on His Heavenly Father. For example, He felt the need for wisdom in decision making, so He went to His Heavenly Father to request it. He needed strength from His Father, so He asked for it during times of miracle-working and when resisting Satan's attacks.

A primary explanation for the amazing power and wisdom seen in Jesus' earthly ministry is that He fully felt His dependence on His Heavenly Father, and He went to that only true Source to be supplied. Jesus prayed not only because He *wanted* to, but also because He *needed* to.

What of Our Prayer Life?

What should be our prayer habits? Let us review some scriptural commands: "Be . . . faithful in prayer" (Romans 12:12). "And pray in the Spirit on all occasions..." (Ephesians 6:18). "Devote yourselves to prayer" (Colossians 4:2). And "pray continually; give thanks in all circumstances, for this is God's will for you in Christ Jesus" (1 Thessalonians 5:17-18).

That is what God's Word commands us to do, but what are our everyday prayer habits really like? Do we pray only when other people are watching or listening? If so, we need to be corrected by the words of Jesus when He said, "When you pray, go into your room, close the door and pray to your Father, who is unseen" (Matthew 6:6). Charles Spurgeon, the well-known nineteenth century pastor of Metropolitan Tabernacle in London, once said in a sermon "If you do not pray alone, you do not pray at all."[7]

Our prayers can be infrequent and anemic. Yet Jesus prayed often, privately, passionately, urgently, and often at length. As devotional writer Andrew Murray confessed, "In His life of sweet prayer, my Savior is my Example."[8]

Why is our prayer life not like the prayer life of Jesus, our Savior and Example? One of the most common excuses is, "I'm too busy to pray." Yet, did not our Lord Jesus lead a busy life? As James Stewart observed, "Busy and crowded as our days are, his were emphatically more so."[9]

Somehow, the excuse *"I'm just too busy to pray"* doesn't seem defensible when we compare ourselves to our Redeemer and model, Jesus Christ. "We make [busyness] a reason for not praying. Jesus made it a reason for praying."[10]

To evaluate truly our own prayerlessness, it would be wise (though perhaps painful) to review Jesus' reasons for leading a life of prayerfulness. If a major reason for Jesus' praying so much is simply that He *wanted* to pray, then isn't it possible that our own prayerlessness reveals *a lack of desire* to pray? A painfully honest reason for not praying is "I really don't feel like it. I really don't want to pray right now."

Prayerlessness, as James Stewart wrote, "is a symptom of something deeper; a symptom of a breakdown of affection."[11] Much of our prayer should be motivated from the desire to commune with God out of the fullness of our hearts, not merely out of our sense of need. If we are praying little, it is quite likely that our love for God has grown cool and our confidence in His love has been forgotten. A lack of communication with God is a sign that the relationship has grown distant, much like the sad relationship of a married couple who rarely have meaningful conversations.

Prayerlessness is often a symptom of a deeper problem, of growing distant from the God who bought us with the blood of His precious Son. Feeling as if we don't want to pray should be the very reason that we must pray! We must draw closer to our Heavenly Father, and in drawing closer, may our relationship be warmed once again. "Let us then approach the throne of grace with confidence, so that we may receive mercy and find grace to help us in our time of need" Hebrews 4:16).

If Jesus spent so much time in prayer because He *needed* to, what does that tell us about our own lack of prayer? Do we think

we really don't *need* to pray? That we can "do it ourselves"? That
we can make it just fine without God's help? As embarrassing as
this is to admit, isn't it true? Might not a major reason for our
prayerlessness be the ugly attitude of self-sufficiency? "Never are
we further from God than when intoxicated by pride."[12] If Jesus
needed to pray "during the days of [His] life on earth," then
imagine how much more we need to make our way into the
throne room of our royal Father daily!

Prayerlessness is not a little problem. It is rarely a problem of
mere busyness or weariness or a lack of discipline. It is usually a
matter of a cool heart or a self-sufficient attitude. It is usually that
we either don't *want* to pray or we think we don't *need* to pray.

Prayerlessness reveals a problem with our core beliefs and
values. Pride and self-sufficiency are at the very heart of sin itself–including the sin of prayerlessness.

What Should We Do about
Our Prayerlessness?

Confess

First, we should confess our prayerlessness to be what it truly
is. It is sin. It is disobedience to those clear commands to pray,
and it is totally unlike our Savior's example. It is only in coming
into the presence of the King of the Universe that our pride is
"chilled and destroyed."[13] Oh, what a comfort it is to know that
"If we confess our sins, he is faithful and just and will forgive us
our sins and purify us from all unrighteousness" (1 John 1:9).

Repent

Next, we need to repent. We need to have a change of thinking
that leads to a genuine change of daily life. When we find ourselves
assuming "We can get along without God on this one," we need to
have a turnaround in our thinking until we say, "Oh, Lord, how
we *need* you. We can do nothing without You!" When we think
we can figure things out on our own, we need to hear the heart-
probing question of God to Job, "Where were you when I laid the
earth's foundation?" (Job 38:4). When we think of ourselves as

self-sufficient, we need to remember the apostle Paul's question, "What do you have that you did not receive?" (1 Corinthians 4:7). When we foolishly think we can go to the world to have our needs met, we must change that thinking. Remember, "Every good and perfect gift is from above" (James 1:17).

Pray

And finally, of course, we need to pray. We must make time to pray. Like our Lord, our lives should be marked by prayer–private, passionate, urgent, and even (at times) lengthy prayer. "Christlike praying in secret will be the secret of Christlike living in public."[14] *"Lord, teach us to pray!"*

> *Arise, my soul, arise,*
> *Shake off thy guilty fears:*
> *The bleeding Sacrifice*
> *In my behalf appears:*
> *Before the throne my Surety stands,*
> *Before the Throne my Surety stands,*
> *My name is written on his hands.*
> *My God is reconciled;*
> *His pardoning voice I hear;*
> *He owns me for his child,*
> *I can no longer fear;*
> *With confidence I know draw nigh,*
> *With confidence I now draw nigh,*
> *And "Father, Abba, Father!" cry.*
> – Charles Wesley

Notes:

[1] James S. Stewart, *The Life and Teaching of Jesus Christ* (New York: Abingdon Press, n.d.), p. 98.

[2] William Garden Blaikie, *Glimpses of the Inner Life of Christ* (London: Hodder & Stoughton, 1876), p. 231.

[3] John A. Broadus, *Jesus of Nazareth* (New York: George H. Doran Co., n.d.), p. 231.

[4] Stewart, p. 102.

[5] Stewart, p. 99.

[6] J. Oswald Sanders, *The Incomparable Christ* (Chicago: Moody Press, 1952), p. 133.

7   Charles Spurgeon, *The Metropolitan Tabernacle Pulpit, Vol. 30* (Pasadena, TX: Pilgrim Publications, 1973 reprint), p. 136.

8   Andrew Murray, *Like Christ* (Philadelphia: Henry Altemus Co., n.d.), p. 133.

9   Stewart, p. 99.

10 James Stalker, *Imago Christi* (New York: American Tract Society, 1889), p. 137.

11 Stewart, p. 99.

12 Stalker, pp. 136-137.

13 Stalker, p. 137.

14 Murray, p. 140.

DISCUSSION QUESTIONS
PRAYING LIKE JESUS DID

1. What characteristics of Jesus' prayer life especially challenge you? Why?

2. Identify the two key reasons Jesus prayed as explained in this chapter.

3. What are some common reasons Christians give for *not* praying? Which of these are legitimate reasons?

4. Describe what you would like your prayer life to be like.

5. What might be some ways your church could encourage church members to grow in their prayer lives? In what ways might you serve your church in encouraging this?

6. If you are married or living in a family context, what might be some ways you can improve your prayer times as a couple or family?

7. If you are not currently doing so, choose a time and place for praying to God daily. Share that commitment with one or two family members or close friends.

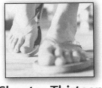

Chapter Thirteen

SERVING
LIKE JESUS DID

The sun was setting as the men gathered for the Passover meal. Many things about the evening would have seemed very familiar to these Jewish men. They found a certain comfort in the familiarity of the Passover elements and liturgy, with which they had all grown up. On the table were the lamb, the unleavened bread, the wine, and the bitter herbs. Yet, mixed with the comfort of the familiar was a certain uneasiness on that spring evening. The buzzing going on around the table seemed somewhat strained. Whispers were floating back and forth among the men gathered for the meal. There was talk of betrayal.

Added to this unsettling discussion was the socially awkward realization that no one had yet performed that common act of hospitality of washing the guests' feet. Sitting off to the side of that upper room was a pitcher and basin, placed next to a long linen towel. Everyone knew the function of those household items. Who would get up to perform the lowly task? The walk from Bethany had been dusty for the 13 men. *Someone* should get up and wash the feet of those present. But who should it be?

Maybe ambitious Peter would pop to his feet and volunteer, or maybe one of the strong silent types, like Andrew the fisherman. Then again, maybe John should do it. After all, he was the youngest. The meal continued in this awkwardness, punctuated with an undercurrent of a debate. As Luke would later record, "A dispute arose among them as to which of them was considered to be greatest" (Luke 22:24).

Without comment, the Master Himself got up. Jesus stood, taking off His outer clothing. Walking toward the pitcher and basin, He wrapped the long linen towel around His waist, suddenly looking very much like a common slave. He got down on His knees and began to work His way around the table, washing and drying the feet of His followers, man by man.

John records this bit of fascinating background before he tells the story of the Master washing the feet of His disciples: "Jesus knew that the Father had put all things under His power, and that he had come from God and was returning to God" (John 13:3). That was John's introductory explanation to his report of Jesus getting up from the meal to wash the disciples' feet.

What was John's point? Jesus was not operating out of a position of weakness, but of power, not out of a position of insecurity, but of certainty. He was secure in His relationship with His heavenly Father. He was confident in His impending return to His place of honor and glory. He was very much aware, also, that the Father had put all things "under His power," or more literally, "into His hands."

So, very much aware of His powerful ability and authority, what did Jesus do? Rather than demanding to *be* served by His followers, Jesus voluntarily chose to serve them! He chose to use His power and authority to serve His men by doing the most menial of jobs—even though His men had been displaying a disturbing pride in their debate and a lack of initiative in serving one another. Why would Jesus do that?

Jesus Was Teaching Them They Would
Need to Be Served by Him

Peter, the outspoken man so many of us relate to, apparently felt the incongruity of having his feet washed by the Master. He protested. Jesus explained to Peter that he needed to humble himself and be washed by Him. In those hours before He went to the cross, Jesus was demonstrating to His disciples that He alone had the power to cleanse them. If they were to be washed spiritually, He alone was qualified. For the men to be His disciples, they would need to humble themselves, and acknowledge their need for cleansing by Jesus. Kneeling by their dirty feet, Jesus explained, "Unless I wash you, you have no part with me" (John 13:8).

Jesus Was Teaching Them to Serve One Another

Jesus was reasoning from the greater to the lesser. It is as though Jesus were explaining it this way: "Men, think for a minute who I am. You call me 'Teacher' and 'Lord.' That's right. That's who I am. Now if I, with my position of power and authority have washed your feet, then you, my followers, should wash one another's feet." John recounts those words that he heard that Passover evening, "I have set you an example that you should do as I have done for you. I tell you the truth, no servant is greater than his master, nor is a messenger greater than the one who sent him. Now that you know these things, you will be blessed if you do them" (John 13:15-17).

Imagine, in that context of men who were arguing as to who was the greatest, it's as though Jesus said, "Quit debating about who is the greatest. Instead, follow my example. Use your ability and authority not to promote yourselves, but to serve one another." Jesus had instructed them less than a week earlier, "You know that the rulers of the Gentiles lord it over them, and their high officials exercise authority over them. *Not so with you.* Instead, whoever wants to become great among you *must be your servant*, and whoever wants to be first *must be your slave*—just as the Son of Man did not come to be served, *but to serve*, and to give his life as a ransom for many" (Matthew 20:25-28, emphasis added).

Has Jesus Washed Me?

Before I can truly serve Jesus or serve other people in His name, I must first submit to His serving me. Have I humbled myself, acknowledging my need to be washed by Jesus? The Son of Man came to serve and to give His life as a ransom for many (Matthew

20:28). Have I been cleansed from the filth of my sin by the Savior? If I would be His follower, I must abandon all my proud attempts to clean up myself, and humbly admit my need to be washed in the blood of the Lamb who was sacrificed at Calvary.

Am I Washing the Feet of Others?

God has given me certain abilities and certain situations in which I have authority over other people. Am I using that authority to promote myself or to serve others? Jesus was clear. He said, "I have set you an example that you should do as I have done for you" (John 13:15). Does my everyday lifestyle indicate that I am walking as Jesus did? Would those who know me best be reminded of Jesus when they watch my life? Does serving others mark my daily walk?

When I think of my life in the workplace or at school, do I mirror the Savior? Have I given in to the temptation to push and shove others out of my way as I seek to climb up the ladder of success? Do my co-workers know me as a person who *uses* people or as someone who *serves* people? Is this true of my relationships not only with people above me, but also of people below me? Am I willing to serve the Lord in my daily work, even if I receive no recognition? Even if someone *else* gets the credit for my work? Is there someone at work or school whose feet the Savior is calling me to wash?

When I evaluate my relationships with others in my church, have I been hanging back waiting to be served, or have I taken the initiative in serving others? Have I been willing to serve only in ministries that receive some form of recognition? Or, have I mirrored the character of my Lord by serving in those less than glamorous ministries such as fixing a meal for a sick person, driving a cancer patient to his oncology treatments, cleaning house for a bereaved church member, or giving a financial gift anonymously? Does my life remind people of Diotrephes who was known in his church as a man "who loves to be first" (3 John 9)? Or, do I remind people of Jesus, who came "not to be served, *but to serve* and give His life"? God has given me abilities and resources to use for His glory in serving others in the church.

How Christlike have I been in serving my brothers and sisters in Christ? Whose feet in my church is Christ calling me to wash?

Often, the place for the real testing of servant-likeness is at home. Do I use my position in the home as a husband, a mother, or an older sibling to demand to be served? Or, like my Lord, do I use my position of authority to serve the others in my home? Is God calling me to serve a disabled or invalid relative? Are there ways I should be encouraging a discouraged relative by my words and actions of kindness? Should I be serving a family member who is overloaded at this time with his or her responsibilities? In what way would Christ want me to "wash the feet" of my spouse, my parents, my children, my siblings this week?

> *Alas, and did my Saviour bleed?*
> *And did my Sov'reign die?*
> *Would He devote that sacred head*
> *For such a worm as I?*
>
> *Was it for crimes that I have done,*
> *He groaned upon the tree?*
> *Amazing pity! grace unkown!*
> *And love beyond degree!*
>
> *Well might the sun in darkness hide,*
> *And shut his glories in,*
> *When Christ, the mighty Maker, died,*
> *For man, the creature's sin.*
>
> *But drops of grief can ne'er repay*
> *The debt of love I owe;*
> *Here, Lord, I give myself away–*
> *'Tis all that I can do!*
>
> - Isaac Watts

DISCUSSION QUESTIONS
SERVING LIKE JESUS DID

1. Read aloud John 13:1-17. What do you think John's purpose was in prefacing the recounting of the footwashing incident with the comments in verses one through three? How might this "preface" impact your life of serving others?

2. Why do you think Peter at first resisted Jesus' attempt to wash his feet? In what ways do you relate to Peter?

3. How would you answer this question: Do my co-workers (or fellow students) know me as a person who *uses* people or as someone who *serves* people? What changes do you believe the Lord wants to work in your life regarding serving others at work or school?

4. Whose feet do you believe the Lord would have you wash (figuratively speaking) in your church? Spend time asking the Lord to direct you to a fellow church member whom you might serve this week.

5. In your home, what are some ways you can reflect Jesus Christ by serving your family members?

6. Spend some time praying, "Lord, make me a Christlike servant." In your prayer, explore with the Lord the various relationships and life situations you have, asking Him to use you in serving others.

7. If you are doing this study in the context of a group, plan a literal footwashing during which you and your fellow group members wash one another's feet, mirroring Jesus' service to His disciples in the Upper Room.

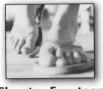

Chapter Fourteen

EXPERIENCING JOY LIKE JESUS DID

Was Jesus a man of joy? Many people picture Jesus as somber—even glum. Indeed, many religious painters have depicted our Lord as sad and gloomy in His demeanor. After all, Isaiah did prophesy that the Messiah would be "a man of sorrows and familiar with suffering" (Isaiah 53:3). Yet, as Princeton theologian, B. B. Warfield suggests in his book *The Person and Work of Christ*, "If our Lord was 'the man of sorrows,' He was more profoundly still 'the man of joy.'"[1] Is it possible to support Professor Warfield's view of a joyful Jesus?

Seeing His Joy

His Situation

Think about some of the situations recorded about Jesus in the Gospel accounts. For example, children were drawn to Jesus (Mark 10:13-16). Have you ever noticed people to whom children gravitate? On whose lap do children feel free to climb? Children are not normally drawn to people who have a sad, sour demeanor. Children are drawn to warm, happy people—to people of joy.

His Actions

The joy of Jesus can also be seen in His participation in festive occasions such as weddings and feasts. Jesus was involved in the wedding of Cana and was also the guest of honor at the party thrown by the newly-converted Matthew. Such participation drew slanderous criticism from some of the dour religious leaders of the day. In His holy disappointment Jesus asked rhetorically, "To what can I compare this generation? They are like children sitting in the marketplaces and calling out to others: 'We played the flute for you, and you did not dance; we sang a dirge, and you did not mourn.' For John came neither eating nor drinking, and they say, 'He has a demon.' The Son of Man came eating and drinking, and they say, 'Here is a glutton and a drunkard, a friend of tax collectors and 'sinners'" (Matthew 11:16-19).

Interestingly, the ministry of Jesus is *contrasted* with the austere and spartan demeanor of John the Baptist's ministry. What might we infer from these spiteful words of contrast by the enemies of Jesus? One man wisely observed, "They are the most precious bits of slander that ever slipped from slimy lips. They prove indisputably that whatever Jesus was not, he was not morose or sour or melancholy."[2]

It is true. When Jesus was present, joy was present! Jesus Himself asked, "How can the guests of the bridegroom mourn while He is with them?" (Matthew 9:15).

Explicit Statements

But we are not limited to interpretations of the *actions* of Jesus. Neither are we limited to possible *allusions* to His being a man of joy. Explicit statements appear in God's Word that Jesus was truly a man of joy. For example, when the 72 "missionaries" returned to Jesus with their encouraging report, it is said that Jesus was *"full of joy"* (Luke 10:21).

Amazingly, the most explicit joyful comments from the lips of the Savior came in the closing hours before His crucifixion. In those hours in the Upper Room with His closest followers, Jesus explained, "I have told you this *so that my joy may be in you* and that your joy may be complete" (John 15:11, emphasis added). Then He prayed to His heavenly Father, "I am coming to you now, but I say these things while I am still in the world, so that they may have *the full measure of my joy* within them" (John 17:13, emphasis added).

After an honest look at the life of Jesus, and a recognition of what He said of Himself as possessing joy, can we really defend the portrait of a gloomy Jesus? Jesus was a man of *joy*. But this recognition stirs up another question. *Why was Jesus a man of joy?*

The Source of Jesus' Joy: Certainty, Not Circumstances

Was Jesus joyful because He lived a pleasant life? Hardly. Jesus knew the normal difficulties of a first-century Palestinian craftsman. Life could be hard. Jesus probably had to labor long hours in His carpenter shop to support His mother and younger half-siblings. Add to those everyday difficulties the pain He encountered in being misunderstood during His ministry years and eventually being rejected by the great majority of His kinsmen. Living in a fallen world with misunderstanding and rejection was a painful experience, no doubt felt more sharply by the sinless Jesus than by a person whose sensitivities were dulled by sin. We cannot explain Jesus' joy by assuming that He lived a life of happy circumstances.

Neither was He joyful because He was somehow anesthetized to pain and disappointment. Robert Law, New Testament professor at Knox College in Toronto, wrote, "No one has ever sounded the depths of reality, has ever penetrated to the ultimate core of life, as Jesus did."[3] Oh, the agony Jesus must have felt, not only from the nails that pierced Him, but also from the horror of being sinless yet becoming sin for us!

Yes, although living the life of a "man of sorrows, and familiar with suffering," Jesus described Himself as a man of *joy* even on the eve of the horrors of His crucifixion. Where did He get such joy in the midst of such pain? In the Bible joy is often linked to faith, hope, and love. Joy is often found in the context of *certainty*—of being *sure*, and Jesus was indeed, *certain*.

His Identity

Jesus was certain of His *identity*. He obviously had a deep assurance of His loving relationship with His heavenly Father. Picture the 30-year-old, dripping wet Jesus standing on the bank of the Jordan River. "As soon as Jesus was baptized, he went up out of the water. At that moment heaven was opened, and He saw the Spirit of God descending like a dove and lighting on Him. And a voice from heaven said, 'This is my Son, whom I love; with Him I am well pleased'" (Matthew 3:16-17). How reassuring those words must have been to Jesus as He moved from the Jordan River to the wilderness to be tempted by Satan. We can only wonder whether Jesus reflected on that moment during the difficulties He experienced in the ensuing months.

Jesus was reassured of His Father's love not only at the beginning of His public ministry, but also toward the end. On the Mount of Transfiguration, Jesus once again was given those comforting words, "This is my Son, whom I love; with him I am well pleased. Listen to him!" (Matthew 17:5).

This link between the assurance Jesus had in His Father's love and His own joy can be most clearly seen in the Upper Room. There, Jesus said to His disciples, "As the Father has loved me, so have I loved you. Now remain in my love. If you obey my commands you will remain in my love, just as I have obeyed my Father's commands and remain in his love. I have told you this *so that my joy may be in you* and that your joy may be complete" (John 15:9-11, emphasis added). Did you hear that? Jesus spoke assuredly of the love the Father had for Him and the love He had for His disciples, then explained that this reminder was to bring *joy* to His followers. The *certainty* of His identity as the much-loved Son of His Father brought Jesus *joy*—even as He contemplated being nailed to the cross in a matter of hours.

His Purpose

The John 15 passage brings out another element of *certainty* that yields *joy*. Jesus said, "I have obeyed my Father's commands" (John 15:10). Jesus repeatedly told others that He was not pursuing His own agenda during His earthly ministry. Rather, He explained that He was "doing the will of my Father." Jesus knew the certainty not only of His personal identity, but He also knew the certainty of what He was doing. Jesus had a certainty of *purpose*. Jesus knew the *joy* of serving His heavenly Father.

Shortly before His arrest, Jesus prayed, "I have brought you glory on earth by completing the work you gave me to do" (John 17:4). Serving *self* brings only a shallow, temporary happiness, but knowing He was doing the will of His heavenly Father brought *real joy* into the earthly life of Jesus.

His Goal

A third element of certainty that contributed to the joy of Jesus is that Jesus *knew where He was going.* Jesus had a confident, forward look. He had a goal placed before Him by His heavenly Father, and pursing that God-given goal brought Jesus joy. He saw His earthly life and ministry from an *eternal* perspective. He saw beyond the weariness, rejection, and pain of this life to the eternal destiny that was laid out for Him. The author of Hebrews wrote, "Let us fix our eyes on Jesus, the Author and Perfecter of our faith, who for the *joy* set before Him endured the cross, scorning its shame, and sat down at the right hand of the throne of God" (Hebrews 12:2, emphasis added).

Jesus was certain of this goal. He had come to this fallen, pain-filled earth to redeem the people His heavenly Father had given Him. Even though the accomplishment of that goal meant enduring the pain and shame of the cross, Jesus pursued the goal with *joy*. In *Glimpses of The Inner Life of Christ*, Free Church of Scotland pastor and professor William Blaikie wrote, "Such a vision of the future, rising out of darkness and confusion of the present, would send a gleam of heaven into the heart of Jesus, and kindle in His countenance a radiance of holy joy."[4]

Summary of Christ's Joy

Pause and reflect on that—Jesus was indeed characterized by *joy*. His joy was not the result of having a life and ministry of pleasant circumstances. Jesus lived life as a "man of sorrows and acquainted with grief." Neither can we find any support for the concept that Jesus was joyful because He had some divine anesthetic against pain. On the contrary, the pure and sinless Jesus surely felt pain *more sharply* than those of us whose emotions have been dulled by our own sin.

Rather, the joy of Jesus is linked in the Bible with the confidence He had in 1) His *identity* as the much-loved Son of God, 2) His *purpose* of doing the will of His Father, and 3) His *goal* of arriving in heaven having accomplished the task the Father had given Him as the Redeemer.

Our Joy

Now, what about us? Should Christians lead lives marked by joy? Some Christians seem to have overreacted to the silly frivolity of our generation by promoting a Christianity that is primarily marked by doom and gloom. These dour Christians give the impression that the more somber the person, the more spiritual he must be. However, as twentieth century philosopher Elton Trueblood wrote in *The Humor of Christ*, "Any alleged Christianity which fails to express itself in cheerfulness, at some point, is clearly spurious."[5] That seems to be a bold statement. Is he right? Let's see.

The Christians described in the New Testament era were marked with joy. The church in Jerusalem "broke bread in their homes and ate together *with glad and sincere hearts*" (Acts 2:46, emphasis added). The picture is one of Christians meeting together with remarkable joy. In fact, the New Testament has repeated *commands* to be joyful. Romans 12:12 says, "Be *joyful* in hope." In the book of Philippians we read, "*Rejoice* in the Lord" (3:1), and "*Rejoice* in the Lord always. I will say it again: *Rejoice!*" (4:4). Similarly, believers in Thessalonica were commanded, "Be *joyful* always" (1 Thessalonians 5:16). Paul explained to the Galatians that "the fruit of the Spirit is...*joy*..." (Galatians 5:22). And He pointed out to the Roman believers that the very "kingdom of God is…righteousness, peace and *joy* in the Holy Spirit" (Romans 14:17). (Emphasis added in the quoted passages.)

The New Testament abounds with portrayals of joyful Christians. In fact, they were *commanded* (as we are) to be joyful. Joy is an identifiable characteristic of one who has been indwelt by the Holy Spirit—of the person who belongs to God's kingdom. Trueblood's assertion is indeed correct. Christianity without joy is spurious.

The Source of Our Joy:
Certainty, Not Circumstances

What is the source of the Christian's joy? Should our joy come from our circumstances? Has God promised us life situations free from pain and frustration? No, the Christian life is marked by trials and troubles. Has God given us some "divine anesthetic" to dull the pain of living in a fallen world? Is this the explanation for Christians having joy? No, we are those who mourn more deeply than our non-Christian neighbors because we are more aware of the painful effects of sin in our lives and in the world (Matthew 5:4). What is the basis of the Christian's joy, then? The believer's joy is like his Master's joy. Just like Jesus, our joy comes from a foundational *certainty—a sureness.*

Our Identity

Like Christ, we Christians have joy because of *the certainty of our identity.* As William Blaikie noted, "Joy depends much less on what we have than on what we are."[6] The knowledge that we are identified as God's chosen children brings the Christian true joy. Jesus instructed, "*Rejoice* that your names are written in heaven" (Luke 10:20, emphasis added). Certain that we who were formerly guilty, condemned sinners are now the forgiven, adopted children of God brings deep joy to the believer.

The forgiven, newly-baptized Ethiopian "went on his way rejoicing" (Acts 8:39). The Philippian jailer "was filled with joy because he had come to believe in God" (Acts 16:34). Enslavement to sin had been turned into freedom in Christ. Condemnation had been turned into salvation. The Father's frown had been turned into a smile. "The religion of Christ is the religion of joy. Christ came to take away our sins, to roll off our curse, to unbind our chains, to open our prison-house, to cancel our debt; in a word, to give us the oil of joy for mourning, the garment of praise for the spirit of heaviness."[7]

We have a new relationship with God. We have a new identity. "Therefore, since we have been justified through faith, we have peace with God through our Lord Jesus Christ, through whom we have gained access by faith into this grace in which we now stand. And we *rejoice* in the hope of the glory of God" (Romans 5:1-2, emphasis added).

Our Purpose

Christians also have joy because of *the certainty of our purpose*. We know that we are servants of the Most High God, and doing what pleases Him floods us with joy. As we obey our heavenly Father, we can know the truth of Oswald J. Smith's song of testimony, *"There is joy in serving Jesus, as I journey on my way."* Pursuing our own pleasure and happiness eventually yields only dryness and disappointment. But pursuing the pleasure of our Lord yields a deep-seated joy. Imagine the joy in every faithful Christian's heart when he hears those most-blessed words on that great day, "Well done, good and faithful servant! You have been faithful with a few things; I will put you in charge of many things. Come and *share your Master's happiness*" (Matthew 25:21, emphasis added).

Our Goal

Like our Lord, Christians know the joy that comes with having *the certainty of where we are headed—a certainty of our goal*. Our lives are not meaningless. Everything that God has providentially brought into our lives is moving us toward His ultimate objective in our lives. Even those painful experiences in life can be met with a profound sense of joy. Paul, who was very experienced in personal suffering, wrote, "Not only so, but we also *rejoice in our sufferings*, because we know that suffering produces perseverance; perseverance, character; and character, hope" (Romans 5:3-4, emphasis added). James echoes Paul in teaching, "Consider it *pure joy*, my brothers, whenever you face trials of many kinds, because you know that the testing of your faith develops perseverance" (James 1:2-3, emphasis added). Seeing that suffering is purposeful, moving us toward God's goal for us, enables us to have true joy. We can see our temporal difficulties in light of the goal of eternity. The words of the Holy Spirit through Peter are most appropriate here:

> *In this you greatly rejoice, though now for a little while you may have had to suffer grief in all kinds of trials. These have come so that your faith—of greater worth than gold, which perishes even though refined by fire—may be proved genuine and may result in praise, glory and honor when Jesus Christ is revealed. Though you have not seen him, you love him; and even though you do not see him now, you believe in him and are filled with an inexpressible and glorious joy, for you are receiving the goal of your faith, the salvation of your souls* (1 Peter 1:6-9).

Our Chief Joy

Furthermore, the Christian has a foundation for joy that exceeds even these three areas of certainty. The Christian has Jesus Christ Himself as his Chief Joy. He is the fountainhead from which flow all other joys. On the night before Jesus was taken away from His disciples for the three days of arrest, trial, crucifixion, and burial, He assured them that their grief would turn to joy. And what would be the motivating force behind their restored joy? "Now is your time of grief, *but I will see you again and you will rejoice*, and no one will take away your joy" (John 16:22, emphasis added). The promised presence of Jesus Christ

Himself is the Christian's *Chief Joy*. As we seek Him and find Him, we have joy.

> *Jesus, I am resting, resting*
> *In the joy of what Thou art;*
> *I am finding out the greatness*
> *Of Thy loving heart.*
> *Thou hast bid me gaze upon thee,*
> *As Thy beauty fills my soul,*
> *For by Thy transforming power,*
> *Thou hast made me whole."*
>   – Jean Sophia Pigott

Notes:

[1] B. B. Warfield, *The Person and Work of Christ* (Philadelphia: The Presbyterian & Reformed Publishing Co., 1950), p. 126.

[2] Charles Edward Jefferson, *The Character of Jesus* (New York: Thomas Y. Crowell Co., 1908), p. 247.

[3] Robert Law, *The Emotions of Jesus*. (Edinburgh: T. & T. Clark, 1915), p. 5.

[4] William Garden Blaikie, *Glimpses of the Inner Life of Christ* (London: Hodder & Stoughton, 1876), p. 222.

[5] Elton Trueblood, *The Humor of Jesus* (New York: Harper & Row, 1964), p. 32.

[6] Blaikie, p. 225.

[7] Octavius Winslow, *The Sympathy of Christ* (Harrisonburg, VA: Sprinkle Publications, 1994), p. 216).

DISCUSSION QUESTIONS
EXPERIENCING JOY LIKE JESUS DID

1. Recount a story about Jesus as found in the Gospels that depicts Him as being joyful. Why are you drawn to this story?

2. Why was Jesus joyful? What were the sources of His joy?

3. What is the source of the Christian's joy?

4. Why do Christians sometimes lack joy?

5. If you feel comfortable doing so, share the story of a time in your life during when you lost your sense of joy. As you reflect on that time, what is it that you may have lost sight of? What has led (may lead) to a regaining of the joy of the Lord in your life?

6. Look up Psalm 51:12. Read the context, and then spend some time making the prayer of this verse your own personal request to the Lord.

Chapter Fifteen

LOVING LIKE JESUS DID

Have you ever wondered what has been the greatest act of love—ever? We can read *The Guinness Book of World Records* and find the *ultimate* example of just about anything: the greatest altitude ever achieved by man, the greatest depth a human being has ever descended into the ocean, the greatest speed ever attained by mankind, and so on. What if *The Guinness Book of World Records* had a category entitled "the greatest act of love?" What entry would we find under that category?

No doubt skeptics would retort, "There's no way anyone could ever decide what the all-time greatest demonstration of love has been!" However, there *is* one particular act of love in history that is the quintessence of love itself—one act of love that makes all other acts of love pale in comparison. There is a specific display that has been declared and documented as being the supreme act of love in the whole history of the human race.

Jesus' Love for Us

God's Word categorically says, "This is how we know what love is: *Jesus Christ laid down His life for us*" (1 John 3:16, emphasis added). The Bible is crystal clear. The all-time act of love that transcends all other demonstrations of love is Jesus' death on the cross in the place of undeserving sinners. What makes Jesus' death on that Roman cross so defining as the ultimate expression of love? What are some of the *qualities* of this supreme demonstration of love?

His Love Was Voluntary

Jesus was *not* a "helpless victim" of the Jewish leaders who manipulated His execution, nor of the Roman soldiers who actually carried out His crucifixion. No one *made* Jesus go to the cross. Jesus willingly *chose* to die on the cross. As recorded in John 10, Jesus Himself explained, "I *lay down* my life for the sheep" (verse 15, emphasis added). *"No one takes it from me,* but I lay it down of my own accord. I have authority to lay it down and authority to take it up again" (verse 18, emphasis added).

Jesus *chose* to die for His sheep because He loved them. This epitome of love, seen in the death of Jesus on the cross, was a purely *voluntary* act.

His Love Was Substitutionary

You and I have to die. When our forefather, Adam, chose to sin against God, death entered the human race.[1] Every sinful human born since then has been "destined to die" (Hebrews 9:27). We know that, unless the Lord returns first, we will all die. Our deaths are the inevitable result of the "sin genes" we inherited from our father, Adam, evidenced in our many, many sins.

However, Jesus did not have to die. As God incarnate, Jesus was the very "author of life" (Acts 3:15). He was the Eternal One walking here on earth as a human being. Jesus was different from all other human beings in this significant way: He had *no sin* (2 Corinthians 5:21, emphasis added).[2] Because He had no sin, Jesus did not have to die.

So, if Jesus didn't *have to* die, why did He? Jesus Himself explained, "I lay down my life *for* the sheep" (John 10:15, emphasis added). That little preposition "for" is so significant. It means "in the place of."[3] Peter later echoed the Savior's explanation for His death when he wrote, "For Christ died for sins once for all, the righteous *for* [same word as in John 10:15] the unrighteous, to bring you to God" (1 Peter 3:18, emphasis added). We sinners deserve to die for our sins, but Jesus took our place on that Roman cross. He died *instead of us.* He died the death you and I should have died. Jesus died *in our place* as an expression of His amazing love.

His Love Was Sacrificial

Jesus' love was more than "talk." He put His love for us in action in the most astonishing way. He sacrificially gave His own perfect, precious life for us. Jesus explained to His followers, "Greater love has no one than this, *that he lay down his life for his friends*" (John 15:13, emphasis added).

Many Christians struggle during times of painful circumstances or emotional depression, asking the soul-searching question, "Does God really love me?" That penetrating question is answered, ultimately, at the foot of the cross. As we recognize the sacrificial death of our Lord, we can be assured of His love for us. He laid down His life for us, and paid the ultimate sacrifice despite our being so undeserving. "You see, at just the right time, when we were still powerless, Christ died for the ungodly. Very rarely will anyone die for a righteous man, though for a good man someone might possibly dare to die. But God demonstrates his own love for us in this: *While we were still sinners, Christ died for us*" (Romans 5:6-8, emphasis added).

His Love Was Personal

Reflect on just how personal the love of the Savior is. Sometimes we are so focused on the parallel truth that "God so loves the world" (John 3:16), that we begin to think of the love of Jesus in merely general terms. Yet, the love Jesus has for us, His followers, is quite *personal*. Who was on Jesus' mind and heart as He prepared to "lay down His life" on the cross? Rather than speculating on the answer, let us listen to Jesus' own declaration. In those anguished hours before the cross, Jesus let His followers eavesdrop on His intercession with His heavenly Father: "I pray for them. I am *not* praying for the world, but *for those you have given me*" (John 17:9, emphasis added).

For those of us who are believers, we can say with grateful confidence, "We were on His heart even as He laid down His life on the cross." We each can repeat personally the words of Paul, "The life I live in the body, I live by faith in the Son of God, *who loved me and gave himself for me*" (Galatians 2:20, emphasis added). Pastor and author John Piper wrote,

> *Surely this is the way we should understand the sufferings and death of Christ. They have to do with me. They are about Christ's love for me personally. It is my sin that cuts me off from God, not sin in*

*general. It is my hard-heartedness and spiritual
numbness that demean the worth of Christ.*

He adds, *My heart is swayed, and I embrace the
beauty and bounty of Christ my treasure. And there
flows into my heart this great reality—the love of
Christ for me. So I say with those early witnesses,
"He loved me and gave himself for me."*[4]

Oh, how He loves you and me!

We revel in the realization that nothing "will be able to separate
us from the love of God that is in Christ Jesus our Lord" (Romans
8:39). The undeserved love Jesus has for us as His followers is more
than just something to be enjoyed. It must be duplicated in our
own lives. Jesus' love for us must have a demonstrable effect on
how we treat one another in the body of Christ.

Our Love for One Another

Christians are to be like their Savior. This is not merely a nice sug-
gestion. It is an obligation. As we have noted from the outset, "This is
how we know we are in him: whoever claims to live in him *must walk
as Jesus did*" (1 John 2:5b-6, emphasis added). This mandatory mirroring of Jesus' character is specifically applied to how we are to love
one another as believers. John recalls Jesus' words, "A new command
I give you: Love one another. *As I have loved you, so you must love one
another*" (John 13:34, emphasis added). As an older man, the apostle
John would explain to his readers, "This is how we know what love
is: Jesus Christ laid down his life for us. *And we ought to lay down our
lives for our brothers*" (1 John 3:16, emphasis added).

Our Love Must be Voluntary

Followers of Christ are under obligation to love one another. Our
Savior has both commanded and modeled this love. Each of us must
submit to our sovereign Savior and choose to obey His commands
daily. And choosing to love certain people can be so difficult at times.

If love by definition is "a sacrificial giving of oneself for the welfare of someone else—even if that other person is *unresponsive or
undeserving,*"[5] then what would motivate us and enable us to love the
unlovely? This is a struggle we all share. New Testament scholar, D. A.

Carson admitted, "The unlovely ones in the brotherhood bring out the worst in me. The whiners get on my nerves. The gossips and the arrogant, the immature and the silly, conspire to drain my resolve."[6]

So, what hope is there that any of us will be able to love those difficult-to-love brothers and sisters (or even family members!)? Frequently, we approach the issue of loving others with an attitude something like this: "I'll love you as long as I *like* you," or "I'll love you as I feel loved *by* you." Let's call this "reactionary love." "As long as I feel sufficiently loved *by* you, I will do my best to love you back, but if I *don't* feel loved enough by you, then I cannot and will not love you." If we rely on other people—spouse, parents, children, brothers and sisters in Christ—to "fill our love tanks" in order to have enough love to give back, we will all quickly find ourselves running on "empty."

There is a much more reliable source for having our "love tanks" sufficiently filled so that we have love for others in turn. The Apostle John explains it this way in 1 John 4, "Dear friends, let us love one another, for love comes from God" (verse 7). "Dear friends, since God so loved us, we also ought to love one another" (verse 11). "And so we know and *rely on*[7] the love God has for us" (verse 16, emphasis added). "We love because he first loved us" (verse 19). Let's call this "overflowing love."

In other words, instead of looking at the "object" of our love as the power source for our love, we must rely on the love we have already received from our Lord. We are "branches" tapped into the "Vine" who is Christ, drawing on His love. Without Him, we can do nothing (John 15:5). Through Him, we can do all things (Philippians 4:13). Knowing and relying on the love the Lord has for us, we can, in turn, voluntarily *choose* to love even the most unlovely person.

Our Love Must Be Substitutionary

Followers of Christ must mirror Jesus' love for us by loving one another in a *substitutionary* way. As we see our brothers and sisters in need, we must, in love, involve ourselves in their lives. Paul stated it this way, "Carry each other's burdens, and in this way *you will fulfill the law of Christ*" (Galatians 6:2, emphasis added). At the heart of the "law of Christ" must be His command "Love each other as I have loved you" (John 15:12).

We must come alongside our brothers and sisters and demonstrate the love of Christ by sharing in their emotional and spiritual struggles, helping them to carry their loads. We can lighten the load our brother or sister is carrying as we walk alongside, supporting, encouraging and loving with a substitutionary love.

Our Love Must Be Sacrificial

Jesus did more than *declare* His love for us in words. He also *demonstrated* His love for us in action—*sacrificial* action. True followers of Jesus Christ will do their best to emulate that kind of Christlike, sacrificial love.

That love can become very practical. John, "the apostle of love," taught, "This is how we know what love is: Jesus Christ laid down his life for us. *And we ought to lay down our lives for our brothers.* If anyone has material possessions and sees his brother in need but has no pity on him, how can the love of God be in him? Dear children, let us not love with words or tongue *but with actions and in truth"* (1 John 3:16-18, emphasis added).

To love others as Christ has loved us, we must not lock the doors of our hearts against those in need. A closed-hearted Christian is an oxymoron! Those who have been loved by Christ will love—must love—their brothers and sisters in tangible, sacrificial ways. When we become aware of needs in the lives of our brothers and sisters, we must willingly share the resources our Lord has entrusted to us. If we have any money, any clothes, any vehicles, any food—whatever—we must be willing to share what we have with those in need.

Our Lord sacrificed His life for us. How sacrificially loving! How can we be stingy when we see our brothers and sisters in material, emotional, or spiritual need? We must live everyday lives remembering the words of our Lord: "Love each other as I have loved you" (John 15:12).

Our Love Must Be Personal

Sometimes we are tempted to love from a distance. We're willing to love others as long as we don't have to get too close. Putting money in the offering plate or sending money to a Christian relief agency seems to salve our consciences. Yet, our consciences should be pricked as we read Paul's counsel to the Romans, "Love must be sincere…Be devoted to one another in brotherly love…Share with God's people who are in need. Practice hospitality…Rejoice with those who rejoice; mourn with those who mourn" (Romans 12:9-15).

Our Lord loved people in a very personal way. He cared about individual people, showing His love to them personally. Recall how He demonstrated love to Levi the tax collector, the woman at the well, the leper, the demon possessed man, Saul of Tarsus—you and me.

As we seek to "love as He loved," should we not also be willing to love people personally? When was the last time you spent time one-on-one with a person struggling with an addiction? A parent who has a rebellious child? A person who lost his job? A brother or sister with a terminal or chronic disease? Let us all commit to love others personally, even as Jesus loved us—even if it moves us out of our comfort zones.

> *See, from His head, His hands, His feet,*
> *Sorrow and love flow mingled down;*
> *Did e'er such love and sorrow meet,*
> *Or thorns compose so rich a crown?*
> *Were the whole realm of nature mine,*
> *That were a present far too small;*
> *Love so amazing, so divine,*
> *Demands my soul, my life, my all.*
> — Isaac Watts

Notes:

[1] Genesis 2:17: "You must not eat from the tree of the knowledge of good and evil, for when you eat of it you will surely die."

[2] On the sinlessness of Jesus, see also Hebrews 4:15; 7:26; 1 Peter 2:22 and 1 John 3:5.

[3] The Greek word in John 10:15 is ὑπερ, which means "instead of," or "in the place of."

[4] John Piper, *The Passion of Jesus Christ* (Wheaton, IL: Crossway Books, 2004), pp. 30-31.

[5] Author's own definition.

[6] D. A. Carson, *The Farewell Discourse and Final Prayer of Jesus* (Grand Rapids, MI: Baker Book House, 1980), p. 103.

[7] The word translated "rely on" in the NIV is literally, "have put our faith in."

DISCUSSION QUESTIONS
LOVING LIKE JESUS DID

1. In your own words, retell the story of one demonstration
   of love from the life and ministry of Jesus that has captured
   your interest. What draws you to this story of Jesus?

2. What are some of the qualities of Jesus' love as seen in
   His death on the cross?

3. As described in this chapter, what is "reactionary love"?
   Why is this type of love so unreliable?

4. Similarly, how does this chapter describe "overflowing
   love"? State the concept of "overflowing love" in your own
   words. Read through 1 John 4:7-21 in formulating your
   answer.

5. Think of a person whom you find especially difficult to
   love. Talk to God about your struggle. Ask Him to give
   you opportunities this week to mirror Christ's love to that
   person.

Chapter Sixteen

THE COST OF WALKING LIKE JESUS DID

The Question

Have you ever watched a Saturday afternoon matinee movie on TV with its annoyingly repetitious and forceful advertisements? "You can get this fabulous ring, made from 'real diamonade' and overlaid with genuine 14 karat gold—for only $19.99! And, if you call *now*, we will also send you this matching set of earrings!" Have you already mailed in *your* $19.99 for your "genuine diamonade" ring? Why not? What's holding you back? Is it because you smell a fake? Who wants a cheap imitation? It's true. Cheap imitations don't cost much. But, then again, they're not worth much either, are they?

Many professing Christians today are like those "diamonade" rings with an "overlay of genuine gold." They look really nice—they seem to have an appearance of Christianity—yet they are nothing more than cheap imitations. Tom Sine wrote, "We all seem to be trying to live the American Dream with a little Jesus overlay. We talk about the lordship of Jesus, but our career comes first. Our house in the 'burbs comes first. Upscaling our lives comes first. Then, with whatever we have left, we try to follow Jesus…and most of us are living lives that *aren't that different from our secular counterparts*"[1] (emphasis added).

Each of us should ask himself, "Am I a genuine Christian? Or, am I a cheap imitation?" It's a sobering question, isn't it? How can we tell? What does a genuine Christian look like, anyway? To answer that, we need to change one crucial word in our question. It's not *what* does a genuine Christian look like, but *Who* does a genuine Christian look like? The Apostle John put it this way: "This is how we know we are in Him: Whoever claims to live in Him *must [*is ob-ligated to*] walk as Jesus did*" (1 John 2:5b-6, emphasis added). Those who truly are in Christ will bear the fruit of living a life like Christ. If someone is not living a Christlike life, his claim of being a Christian is bogus. A genuine Christian looks like Jesus as he goes through daily life. He walks the kind of walk that Jesus walked.

The Call

Jesus stands before us, even as He stood before that Galilean crowd, and calls out, "Come to me, all you who are weary and bur-dened, and I will give you rest. Take my yoke upon you and *learn from me*, for I am gentle and humble in heart, and you will find rest for your souls" (Matthew 11:28-29, emphasis added). The gra-cious King commands us to step out of the crowd and come learn from Him. As we come to Jesus, we see Him bearing the character traits of meekness, servant-likeness, compassion, joy, holiness, and so on. As He gives us new life, we must begin to bear these same Christlike marks in our lives. Meekness, servant-likeness, compas-sion, joy, holiness, and more must mark us, too. Will we step out from the crowd of lost humanity and take our stand with Jesus? As He gives us new life, are we ready and willing to pay the required cost of a Christlike life?

The Cost

What is the cost of following Jesus Christ? The answer seems like a paradox. On the one hand, following Jesus costs us *nothing*. As Paul wrote in Romans 6:23, "the *gift* of God is eternal life in Christ Jesus our Lord" (emphasis added). Becoming a Christian doesn't cost us anything. There's nothing we can pay to acquire eternal life. It is purely a free gift from God.

However, on the other hand, following Jesus will cost us *ev-erything*. Jesus Himself laid out this cost of total commitment. He challenged people who were contemplating becoming His fol-lowers, "If anyone comes to me and does not hate his father and mother, his wife and children, his brothers and sisters—yes, even his own life—he cannot be my disciple. And anyone who does not carry his cross and follow me cannot be my disciple" (Luke

14:26-27). After illustrating the urgency of counting the cost, he reasserted, "Any of you who does not give up everything he has cannot be my disciple" (Luke 14:33).

So, if we are going to heed the call of Jesus to come learn from Him, we must count the cost. Committing ourselves to living a Christlike life will cost us everything. To think through this cost in more detail, let's look at Jesus' bold declaration in Luke 9:23. He unapologetically explained, "If anyone would come after me, he must deny himself and take up his cross daily and follow me."

The Cost of Self-Denial

First, Jesus said that if we are going to follow Him, we must *deny* ourselves. What did He mean by that? He did not mean denying things *to* ourselves, the way some people give up candy or smoking for Lent. Jesus isn't calling on His followers to give up certain objects or activities. The "*thing*" He is demanding that we give up is *ourselves!* We must no longer live for our *selves.* No more living for *self*-promotion, *self*-defense, *self*-esteem, or *self*-fulfillment. No longer can we live a life of demanding our rights and our own ways. No longer can we live lives committed to the pursuit of *our own* happiness. We must renounce our *selves.* We must turn our backs on *self* and *selfishness.*

The Cost of Death to Self

Second, we must "take up our cross daily." Now, what does that mean? The cross is more than a symbol of inconvenience. Many people would call their arthritis, difficult boss, or lazy husband "my cross to bear." But what Jesus means here is more than an inconvenience. The cross is a symbol not only of suffering, but of *death*. Following Jesus Christ—committing ourselves to living Christlike lives—will require that we take up our symbol of death. Every day of our lives, we must take up our symbol of death, signifying that we no longer live for our old desires and our old lifestyles. We no longer live for our *selves.* Isn't this Paul's testimony in Galatians 2:20, "I have been crucified with Christ and I no longer live, but Christ lives in me"?

The Cost of Daily Following

And third, we must *follow* Christ. We "must walk as Jesus did." We must go *His* way and not our own. We must not deviate from the path down which He is leading us. We cannot go to the right or to the left, but must keep following after our glorious leader. Isn't it interesting that one of the most basic descriptions one can give for a Christian is "a *follower* of Jesus Christ?" Yet, there are many people in western Christianity who claim to be Christians, but whose daily life is following a far different path from the one Jesus walked. It is terrifying to think of the many imitation Christians who will hear those horrifying words from the lips of King Jesus on Judgment Day, "I never knew you. Away from me, you evildoers!" (Matthew 7:23). *Oh Lord, by your grace, may I not be in their number!*

The Commitment

Jesus Christ calls us to come *learn* from him—to come *follow* him. To do that means that we must live Christlike lives. *We must walk as Jesus did.* To do so will cost us. It will cost us everything. Will we pay the price? Will we make that commitment? As we contemplate this most important question, let us tune our ears once more to the words of King Jesus. We must weigh these words carefully: "For whoever wants to save his life will lose it, but whoever loses his life for me will save it. What good is it for a man to gain the whole world, and yet lose or forfeit his very self?" (Luke 9:24-25).

Do we understand the *warning* Jesus is giving us? If we decide that denying ourselves is too costly—if we decide that dying to ourselves is too much to pay—then we will be making an eternally damning choice. By choosing to hang onto our *own* lives, by deciding to live for our *selves–self-promotion, self-protection, self-assertion, self-happiness*–we will, by that choice, actually be forfeiting our own souls.

Jesus will not be content with our lives if we merely *claim* to be Christians while, in fact, we are living lives following our own pursuits. Despite our verbal claims, He will see right through the cheap overlay of our lives. He will see by our lifestyles that we are still living for ourselves. He will see by our lifestyles that in actuality we are denying Him. And on that most-important day, He will deny us. By seeking to hang onto what this world has to offer us, we will, in fact, be choosing to forfeit our souls. What good is that? What an eternally foolish choice! No, we must not choose that way!

Instead, we must take to heart the great promise of our Lord. If, in faith, we will truly heed His word, we will willingly—gladly—lose our lives for Him. We will turn our backs on the various paths this world calls us to follow. Those paths may seem right. They may promise life, but they end in death (Proverbs 14:12). Following those paths may look promising, but we know from our Lord that they actually end in hell. Instead, we must abandon our *selves*. In doing so, He will give us new life. He will energize us to follow Him. In making the commitment to follow Him—to live Christ-empowered, Christlike lives—we will be given eternal life.

The Conclusion

"This is how we know we are in him: whoever claims to live in him must walk as Jesus did" (1 John 2:5b-6). Jesus has called us to come *learn* of Him. Like the apostle Paul, may we have the God-given, lifelong passion that bursts forth with, "I want to know Christ!" (Philippians 3:10). Jesus has called us to come *follow* Him. Doing that will cost us everything. But in losing our lives, we will actually find them. We will find that in dying to ourselves, our gracious Lord will give us His life. And the fruit of that gift will be that our lives will bear His character. *We will walk as Jesus walked.*

> *More like the Master, I would ever be,*
> *More of His meekness, more humility;*
> *More zeal to labor, more courage to be true,*
> *More consecration for work He bids me do.*
> *Take Thou my heart*
> *I would be Thine alone;*
> *Take Thou my heart*
> *and make it all Thine own;*
> *Purge me from sin,*
> *O Lord, I now implore,*
> *Wash me and keep me*
> *Thine forevermore.*
> – Charles H. Gabriel

Note:
[1] Sine, Tom., "Will the Real Cultural Christians Please Stand Up," *World Vision* (Oct./Nov. 1989).

DISCUSSION QUESTIONS
THE COST OF WALKING LIKE JESUS DID

1. According to 1 John 2:5b-6, what is a key identifying mark of a true Christian?

2. In your own words, explain the phrase, "Take up your cross daily." What does it cost to follow Jesus Christ?

3. Without becoming spiritually abusive, how can our churches be more faithful in warning people of the danger of being mere "imitation" Christians?

4. Have you been convicted by the Holy Spirit that you have been living a lie? That you are, to this point in your life, not a true follower of Jesus Christ, but in fact, a mere "imitation" with a little Jesus overlay? Read Matthew 11:28-29. Will you this day obey the gracious command of King Jesus to come to Him, asking Him to do His work of saving grace in your life?

5. What changes in your commitment to follow Christ do you feel the Holy Spirit has been laying on your heart? Take the words of Charles H. Gabriel's poem (found at the end of this chapter) and make them your personal prayer to God.

6. Commit to memorizing 1 John 2:5b-6. In one week, repeat this verse aloud to your study group or to an accountability partner.

Chapter Seventeen

THE REWARD OF WALKING LIKE JESUS DID

"What do you want to be when you grow up?" Many of us have asked children that question as a means of getting to know them. I remember one time asking a little boy that question, and he looked at me and said with great enthusiasm, "When I grow up, I want to be a *man*!" Not a bad goal for a little boy, is it?

Maybe we shouldn't leave that question in the realm of children. No matter what our current age, we each should consider the question, "What do you want to be when *you* grow up?" More precisely, "What do you want to be when you grow up *spiritually*?"

Then again, maybe we should re-phrase the question. Suppose we were asked, "*Who* do you want to be like when you *grow up spiritually*?" We all want to grow into spiritual maturity, but isn't spiritual maturity better defined in *who* terms rather than in *what* terms? A Christian growing in spiritual maturity looks more and more like Jesus.

Isn't that the heart's desire of every true follower of Christ—*to be more like Jesus*? English pastor and writer John Stott wrote these heart-stirring words, "We are not interested in skin-deep holiness, in a merely external resemblance to Jesus Christ…No, what we long for is a deep inward change of character, resulting from a change of nature and leading to a radical change of conduct. In a word, we want to be *like Christ*, and that thoroughly, profoundly, entirely. *Nothing less than this will do*" (emphasis added).[1]

If Christlikeness is our heart's desire—our life-long quest, *how* does that happen? How does a Christian grow to be more and more like Jesus? By what process can a Christian more and more reflect the character and actions of Christ in his or her life? How is Christlikeness worked out in the life of a Christian?

The Bible gives answers to that important question in 2 Corinthians 3:18, "And we, who with unveiled faces all reflect the Lord's glory, are being transformed into his likeness with ever-increasing glory, which comes from the Lord, who is the Spirit." Let us focus on two key words in this verse—*changing* and *reflecting*.

Changing

All who have put their faith in Jesus Christ are in the process of being changed. The clear implication is that we *need* to be changed from what we currently are to what we should be. In our most honest moments, believers freely acknowledge our need for change. We all still have sin in our lives, and some of those sins seem to cling to us persistently. We all recognize various aspects of spiritual immaturity in our lives. We *want* to be changed. We *need* to be changed.

This leads us to ask, "Into what kind of people are we being changed?" What is God doing with us? God's involvement in our lives is purposeful. "And we know that in *all things* [both the painful and the pleasurable experiences in life] God works for *the good* of those who love him, who have been called according to his purpose" (Romans 8:28, emphasis added). And what is that "good" that God is working into our lives? "For those God foreknew *he also predestined to be conformed to the likeness of his Son*" (Romans 8:29, emphasis added). *That* is the goal. God planned a goal ahead of time for us, and that goal is Christlikeness.[2]

Sometimes people say, "I just want to be myself." However, for those of us who profess to be followers of Jesus Christ, our aspiration must be greater than merely "being myself." We have a higher purpose, and that is to be like Jesus—to reflect His character—to "walk as Jesus did." As poet Thomas Chisholm expressed in his hymn, "I have one deep, supreme desire, that I may be like Jesus. To this I fervently aspire, that I may be like Jesus."[3]

The goal of Christian maturity is Christlikeness. Jesus is the model of what we Christians are to become. The "first Adam" rebelled against the Creator, and brought sin and its damaging effects on the whole human race. As our representative, that first man, Adam, "messed up" God's design for His image bearers. Human beings were made to reflect God's glory in ways not seen in any other created thing. However, because of Adam's sin, that created purpose of perfectly reflecting God's glory went unfulfilled in the human race.

Then Jesus came. He came to this earth as a real human being, perfectly reflecting the Father's glory. "The Son is the radiance of God's glory and the exact representation of his being" (Hebrews 1:3).[4] Jesus, the perfect, sinless man, serves as the prototype of what God will do with all His redeemed people. Just as the "first man," Adam, brought sin and death to the human race, the "second man," Jesus Christ, brought redemption and life. "The first man was of the dust of the earth, the second man from heaven. As was the earthly man, so are those who are of the earth; and as is the man from heaven, so also are those who are of heaven. And just as we have borne the likeness of the earthly man, *so shall we bear the likeness of the man from heaven*" (1 Corinthians 15:47-49, emphasis added).

When Jesus returns to this earth, that transformation will be completed. The apostle John assures us, "Dear friends, now we are children of God, and what we will be has not yet been made known. But we know that when he appears, *we shall be like him, for we shall see him as he is*" (1 John 3:2, emphasis added). From that glorious moment of ultimate transformation, we redeemed image bearers will finally fulfill our mission of perfectly reflecting God's glory by ruling and reigning over the new heavens and new earth as God's representatives.[5]

But, what about *now*? We anxiously await "graduation day" when that final transformation will be accomplished in us. Meanwhile, what is God doing in our lives? 2 Corinthians reminds us that this change is already in process. We *are being transformed into his likeness*" (2 Corinthians 3:18, emphasis added). This transformation is not the result of some self-improvement plan. The change does not come about merely through our own efforts. Being transformed into Christlikeness is the work of the Holy Spirit in the lives of believers. As the apostle Paul notes in this verse, this change "comes from the Lord, who is the Spirit."

In 2 Corinthians 3, Paul uses the analogy of a veil covering a person's face to depict an unredeemed person's inability to understand spiritual things. He speaks of this spiritual "veil" when he observes, "It has not been removed, because only in Christ is it taken away" (2 Corinthians 3:14). Then the apostle assures us, "But whenever anyone turns to the Lord, the veil is taken away. Now the Lord is the Spirit, and where the Spirit of the Lord is, there is freedom" (2 Corinthians 3:16).

The Holy Spirit draws us to Christ and "takes the veil off" our minds and hearts, so we can see Christ as Savior and Lord. He "gave us ears and gave us eyes."[6] No longer are we spiritually blind and insensitive to Christ. The Holy Spirit reveals Christ to us not just at our conversion experience, but *daily*. The Holy Spirit is Christ-revealing and Christ-promoting in His ministry to us.[7] As He daily continues to reveal Jesus Christ to us, we are changed—transformed.

What does that transformation process look like? It is not instantaneous, but gradual and sure. In fact, our English word "metamorphosis" comes from the Greek word that is translated "transformed" in this verse. "Metamorphosis" implies a gradual, but sure, change from one form to another. For example, when I was a boy, my cousins and I loved to go to a little pond on our grandparents' property. In the spring we would see tiny tadpoles swimming around near the edges of the pond. We would try to catch some and put them in a jar to watch for a while. Maybe a week or two would go by before we returned to our grandparents' home and continued our adventure at the pond. But on our return, as we lay on our bellies on the grass by the edge of the water, we would notice how our little tadpoles had become big tadpoles—with those strange-looking legs beginning to sprout from their bulbous bodies. By the beginning of summer, our tadpole friends could no longer be found swimming in the shallows. Instead, we would find frogs leaping into the water as we approached the pond's edge. The tadpoles had gradually, but surely, been changed by that process we call "metamorphosis" to become like their frog parents who gave them life.

Similarly, the Holy Spirit brings about "metamorphosis" in our lives, gradually and surely changing us to become more like Jesus, who has given us new birth. 2 Corinthians 3:18 says that change is "with ever-increasing glory" (NIV). That phrase could be translated literally "from glory to glory." The idea is that the Holy Spirit is changing us *progressively*. He is taking Christians from one stage to the next in Christlikeness. Sometimes He leads us in a "baby step" in the transformation process, and sometimes He leads us in a giant step. Either way, He is always bringing us in a sure progression "until Christ is formed" in us (Galatians 4:19).

Christians sometimes lose sight of this gradual metamorphosis that the Holy Spirit is working in our lives. We want change *now*. However, we shouldn't become impatient or discouraged. It would be a good exercise for each Christian to stop and reflect just how far the Holy Spirit has brought him thus far in his Christian walk. Maybe we should have the spirit of the rough-hewn Christian man who said, "I might not be what I *will* be, and I might not be what I *want* to be, but praise God, *I'm not what I used to be!*" Amen.

It is encouraging to acknowledge the work of the Holy Spirit who is gradually, but surely, changing us to become more and more like Jesus. But *how* does He do it? What process does He use to bring about that change toward Christlikeness? Consider a second key word in 2 Corinthians 3:18.

Reflecting

The Greek word translated in the NIV as "reflecting" is a bit of a challenge for the translators. In some places it seems to have the idea of "contemplating"—of looking at something intently and thoughtfully.[8] In other places, this same participle carries the idea of "reflecting" or "mirroring back what is shining on it." Both translations are attractive.

We "contemplate" Jesus Christ as the Holy Spirit removes that veil of spiritual darkness, so we can see Jesus in all His glory and grace. "The god of this age has blinded the minds of unbelievers, so that they cannot see the light of the gospel of the glory of Christ, who is the image of God…For God, who said, 'Let light shine out of darkness,' made his light shine in our hearts to give us the light of the knowledge of the glory of God in the face of Christ" (2 Corinthians 4:4 and 6).

Some people were given the privilege of seeing the glory of Jesus Christ "in the flesh." Peter testified, "We were eyewitnesses of His majesty" (2 Peter 1:16). Similarly, John attested, "We have seen His glory, the glory of the One and Only, who came from the Father, full of grace and truth" (John 1:14).

However, this privilege of "contemplating" Jesus Christ is true even for those of us who have not seen Jesus with our physical eyes. As we read the Word of God as believers, the Holy Spirit glorifies the Son in our minds and hearts (John 16:14). As we pray and worship, the Holy Spirit brings us before our Lord Jesus, stirring our minds and hearts so that we stand amazed in His presence. As we suffer, the Holy Spirit draws us closer to Christ so that we can contemplate Him and His work for us.

We also begin to "reflect" Jesus Christ as we "contemplate" Him. When Moses went up Mount Sinai, he was exposed to the glory of God. As he was in the presence of God, he began to "reflect" His glory.[9] As Christians, we have the same privilege Moses had. With unveiled hearts, we look at Jesus Christ and see His glory. As we do, we increasingly "reflect" His glory in our own lives. As we are being transformed, the glory of Jesus is progressively seen in us. We become moons reflecting the glory of the Son. We increasingly reflect His character. His meekness is progressively produced in us. His compassion is seen more and more in our lives. His joy is increasingly evident in our daily

walk. His love is more and more evident in our own relationships. Praise the Lord!

The world takes note of this metamorphosis. For example,
when the apostles Peter and John were arrested and forced to
appear before the body of religious leaders in Israel, the San-
hedrin members were amazed at their demeanor. "When they
saw the courage of Peter and John and realized that they were
unschooled, ordinary men, they were astonished and *they took
note that these men had been with Jesus*" (Acts 4:13, emphasis
added).

Many Christians can testify to receiving similar reactions
from friends and family who were acquainted with them before
they came to know Christ. As the Holy Spirit continues to do His
transforming work in the life of the follower of Christ, friends,
family and acquaintances often remark on the notable changes
in the believer. Our *verbal* testimony for Christ is strengthened
by our *visible* testimony. As the Holy Spirit continues to make us
more and more like Jesus, we increasingly reflect His character in
our own lives. This metamorphosis is like a dimmer switch being
turned up brighter and brighter. May each of us be ablaze with
the glory of Christ!

Conclusion

The question is not so much "*What* does Christian maturity look like?" as it is "*Who* does Christian maturity look
like?" *Christian maturity looks like Jesus Christ.* We want this
Christlikeness to be seen in our lives in increasing measure. May
each of us spend time with Jesus Christ as we thoughtfully gaze
at Him in His Word as we read it ourselves and as we hear it
taught and preached. Let us spend time in prayer, enjoying the
fellowship with Him and asking the Holy Spirit to continue His
transforming work in our lives. Let us devote ourselves to God-
honoring, Christ-exalting worship, not being content with "it's-
all-about-me" worship. Let us not "waste" the suffering that God
sovereignly brings into our lives, but realize that suffering is His

means of polishing the mirror of our lives so that we are better reflectors of His glory.

"Lord, change me. Make me more like Jesus."

> *But grow in the grace and knowledge*
> *of our Lord and Savior Jesus Christ.*
> *To him be the glory both now and forever! Amen"*
> *- 2 Peter 3:18*

Notes:

[1] John Stott, *Focus on Christ* (New York: Collins Publishers, Inc., 1979), p. 153.

[2] Also see 1 Corinthians 15:49: "...so shall we bear *the likeness of the man from heaven*" (emphasis added). Also, Galatians 4:19, "My dear children, for whom I am again in the pains of childbirth *until Christ is formed in you...*" (emphasis added).

[3] Thomas Chisholm, "I Want to Be Like Jesus" found in *The Hymnal for Worship and Celebration* (Waco, TX: Word Music), hymn 400. (Note: copyright 1945. Renewed 1973 by Lillenas Publishing Co.)

[4] Is this not the point of the author of Hebrews in chapter 2? He writes of God's design for the human race. He says of human beings that God "crowned him with glory and honor and put everything under his feet" (verses 7-8, quoting Psalm 8). He confirms, "In putting everything under him [that is, the human being], God left nothing that is not subject to him" (verse 8). He then makes this painfully true observation about God's "job description" for human beings still being unfulfilled, "Yet, at present we do not see everything subject to him." The first Adam and all his descendants have yet to fulfill their God-given mandate to reflect His glory on this earth by ruling and reigning on His behalf. While we are contemplating this sad realization of our unfulfilled mission, the author of Hebrews then draws our attention to the one human being who has indeed fulfilled the God-given mission for us image bearers. He assures, "But we see Jesus" (verse 9).

[5] The last chapter in the Bible tells us that we "will reign for ever and ever" (Revelation 22:5). In Revelation 1:5, Jesus is called "the ruler of the kings of the earth" [that is, His redeemed and glorified people].

[6] From John Newton's hymn "*Let us Love, and Sing, and Wonder,*" (in public domain).

[7] See John 16:14: "He will bring glory to me by taking from what is mine and making it known to you."

[8] See the NIV text note on this verse.

[9] Exodus 34:29 reports, "When Moses came down from Mount Sinai with the two tablets of the Testimony in his hands, he was not aware that his face was radiant because he had spoken with the LORD."

DISCUSSION QUESTIONS
THE REWARD OF WALKING LIKE JESUS DID

1. What is God's ultimate goal for Christians? Share at least one Bible passage to support your answer.

2. According to 2 Corinthians 3:17-18, what is the role of the Holy Spirit in the process of our maturing as Christians?

3. What are some of the processes the Holy Spirit uses in transforming us to be more like Jesus?

4. How can churches be more intentional in encouraging members to become more Christ-focused as a way of life? What role does worship have? The preaching and teaching of the church? The "values" depicted in the life of the body?

5. Do you have a daily time of reading God's Word and reflecting on Christ? If not, will you make a commitment to begin that discipline of grace in your life? Will you share that commitment with your discussion group or with an accountability partner?

6. Think back over your Christian experience since God saved you. What are some of the changes the Holy Spirit has worked in your life to make you more like Jesus? Take some time and thank Him for His transforming work in your life. Ask Him to continue to make you more like Jesus.